SKYDIVING
FOR
PARENTS

Raising amazing kids without going into free fall

Jane Bullivant

MONARCH
BOOKS

Oxford, UK & Grand Rapids, Michigan, USA

First published in the UK in 2006 by Monarch Books
(a publishing imprint of Lion Hudson plc),
Mayfield House, 256 Banbury Road, Oxford OX2 7DH.
Tel: +44 (0)1865 302750 Fax: +44 (0)1865 302757
Email: monarch@lionhudson.com
www.lionhudson.com

ISBN-13: 978-1-85424-727-8 (UK)
ISBN-10: 1-85424-727-1 (UK)
ISBN-13: 978-0-8254-6124-8 (USA)
ISBN-10: 0-8254-6124-3 (USA)

Distributed by:
UK: Marston Book Services Ltd, PO Box 269,
Abingdon, Oxon OX14 4YN;
USA: Kregel Publications, PO Box 2607,
Grand Rapids, Michigan 49501

British Library Cataloguing Data
A catalogue record for this book is available from the British Library.

Printed and bound in Great Britain by Cox & Wyman Ltd, Reading

Contents

Introduction   5

1   Kick-starting your parenting 'va-va-voom'   7

2   This isn't the kid I ordered!   19

3   Ditching your baggage   35

4   How to turbo-boost your kid's self-esteem   47

5   Rebooting your kid's imagination   65

6   For your eyes only   83

7   Parenting hot potatoes   99

8   Having it all – is it really possible?   115

9   Around the kitchen table...   133

Introduction

Welcome to *Skydiving for Parents*, the book. I'm so glad you've dropped by. Kick off your world-weary shoes, pour yourself a huge mug of hot chocolate with those mint sprinkly bits on top, and let me give you a preview of what's in store...

This book is about escaping juggling overload and living life to the full. It's about reclaiming parenting from the 'TO DO' list and achieving the family life of your dreams. Each chapter explores the tried and tested ways to raise great kids and build an awesome family life.

There are plenty of books out there on how to life-laundry your world, colour-code your calling, de-clutter your diary. This book is NOT about getting all the perfect answers and whipping life into order. Family life is just too sticky for that – there are pet hamsters to catch, Lego to be kicked under the sofa, socks to match. This book contains real-world encouragement gleaned from experienced parents, the world over. It's about enjoying the parenting journey, making great choices and... raising the most amazing kids (yours!).

1

Kick-starting your parenting 'va-va-voom'

All I wanted was to nip into the pharmacy, buy shampoo, and get out. Yet with a gaggle of bored kids in tow, a mobile yelping for attention and cute new shoes nipping at my feet, my chances of achieving coconut bouncing locks were diminishing by the second. Pausing in the shopping mall to locate my mobile somewhere in the crumb-caked crevice of my bag, two of my kids attached themselves onto my feet like giant kid slippers. Phone between my teeth, I shuffled into the store, grabbed the nearest shampoo (yep, I'm the sucker who bought the 'ginger, nutmeg and essence of musk'). Standing in the queue, I dished out raisins to the tribe, put a soggy biscuit in a nearby bin and made a mental note to buy fish food. Nearly done...

Juggling? I'm a master. I can bake, do my kids' algebra, plan Christmas, do my nails, all while sympathising over my friend's dead cat. But do you know what? Juggling sucks. Maybe I've been the last to catch on, but this juggling business has a large downside. You see, I find myself never really living in the moment, and always thinking two steps ahead on the mental tick list. It's not that I don't enjoy a challenge; it's just the franticness of it all that really sucks.

You might have guessed I'm no neatly tweaked parenting author lazing on a hammock, sipping chilled lemonade as the dog snoozes at my feet. I'm actually wedged on the sofa *avec* laptop and a crème egg watching a re-run of *Who Wants to be a Millionaire?* It was a toss-up between that and *Supernanny*, and those parenting programmes make me feel so guilty. There is no dog snoozing at my feet; our family pet is a snail called Virgil 2 who is the sole reason I spend half my life crawling around on the floor (this sucker moves fast). I'm a just a mum who has lots of fun, makes lots of mistakes and spends her days chasing after three turbocharged kids and stuffing more food into a freezer than is humanly possible. There are a few things I do know for sure. I know I love my family more than I ever thought could be possible. I love life, and I want us to embrace it, go the whole hog. Having emerged from eight years of being pregnant, breastfeeding or being a night-time snuggle buddy, I may have a touch of sleep-induced delirium but I want our family life to be rich, vibrant, alive, full of adventure. I've read plenty of 'have it all' books, and certainly gleaned some great tips on the art and science of juggling. Nevertheless, I have a sneaky feeling that if I keep treating life as one big itinerary I might just find myself so busy jumping the waves that I miss the sunset.

If I were honest, I'd very much like to put the blame for the relentless pace of 21st century parenthood firmly in the lap of a society which expects a parent to be superhuman. Nevertheless, between you and me, I know that I'm just as much to blame for not cutting myself some slack. Take yesterday, for example; due to a freak set of coincidences I actually had a Saturday afternoon to myself. What to do? Run myself a well-deserved hot bath or get the ironing out the way/load the dishwasher/find the escapee snail/match a mountain of socks? I know I should choose the bath (I know, I know), but the lure of being ahead of the game is sometimes too hard to resist. The socks win hands down.

The bottom line is that squeezing more into life than should ever be possible doesn't deliver on the satisfaction front. Most of us multi-task not because we are control freaks, or irreparably disorganised, but because we want to have a great life. Well, I have scoured the world for the answers on how to raise great kids AND escape juggling overload. I've spoken to famous child-rearing experts, adopting mums, grandmothers, mums from all corners of the world, a mum of eleven, and even a tribal chief. Through my quest for parenting know-how, I've been contacted through magazines, online parenting forums and national newspapers. Amazingly, many people offered the same four pearls of wisdom for laying the foundation for a great family life. The rest of this chapter is devoted to these four glossy pearls of inspiration and encouragement that will kick-start your parenting 'va-va-voom' like never before. Then, the rest of the book explores further precious jewels of wisdom gleaned from worldwide parents and my own crazy parenting adventure. Dive in, friend!

Wisdom pearl number 1: The de-cluttering myth

Pick up any glossy home-interiors magazine and laced somewhere in the seductive pages will be the words 'the kitchen is the heart of the home'. Well, that's not the case in our house. For us, it's the fridge. Maybe this is because that's where the cupcakes are stashed, or because if you reach up onto the top and rummage around you might just get lucky and find some lost coins or a forgotten packet of cookies. I guess the fact that the fridge cossets the stash of ready meals may have something to do with it. Try as I might to attain the apple-pie-baking perfection of my mum, I'm still more of a microwave meal vixen given half a chance. Our fridge is chrome, not that I've seen the surface for a while as the fridge has always been the place I stick really important things: soccer schedules, splatter paint masterpieces, money-off coupons, bills... you know the sort of stuff. Well, the magazines say de-cluttering is the 'new black', so if I were going to step off the hamster wheel of life, first base, I assumed, would be to get organised. A few schedules and systems would whip things into shape, surely. With the vigour of a 1950s mom in an apron, I set to work sorting the huge array of fridge paraphernalia decorating the door. Three bags of trash later, it was sorted. Schedules all magnetised to the fridge, job done. Yet, rather than a smug satisfaction at my veritable office of a fridge door, I felt slightly unsettled. I fleetingly wondered if the flurry of activity was actually of much value at all. I was already on 'hyper mode' keeping on top of everything with an eye on the clock ready to move onto the next thing. Would MORE schedules ease the stress? Or would that elusive thing called inner calm slip out of my grasp yet again?

A few weeks later, whilst trying to reach under the fridge in a vain attempt to locate my son's glow-in-the-dark lightsabre, I pulled out a few screwed-up leaflets that had escaped my clear-out and languished under the fridge. One was a fragrance promotion leaflet from the local beauty store. Words such as 'Allure', 'Eternity', 'Intoxicating', 'Passion', 'Eden' and 'Captivate' dripped off the page like liquid gold. Crouched on the floor, arm wedged under the fridge, I realised that a 'liquid gold' quality of family life was going to take something more than a smidge of effort and a few schedules. I knew for sure that the answer was NOT to burn out attempting dizzy heights of super-organisation.

Child rearing is an unknown journey, full of twists and turns. Having an organised 'plan' and schedule neatly mapped out can give a fantastic sense of control and inner calm. Nevertheless, relying on this too much can leave a parent out of their depth when something unexpected happens (which is pretty inevitable). The further risk of managing life too tightly is that your relationship with your kids starts to feel more like 'manager' and 'employee', than parent and child. Family relationships are just too precious to be exchanged for a fleeting sense of control.

Organisation is a very useful tool; it's not the goal. This simple pearl of wisdom was one of the most cherished by many mums who contacted me. Older mums said how they wished they had spent less time managing life with children, and more time enjoying life with children. One Australian mum expressed it well: 'First base for me was resisting the urge to think that being organised was the answer to everything. I could be the most organised person in the world, but it wouldn't necessarily make everything right. Making better choices with things was what made a real difference for me.'

Wisdom pearl number 2: The 'G' word

My childhood veered wildly between wading through streams with slimy frogs clutched between my fingers, and flouncy polka dot skirts and lemon clip-on earrings. One great memory I have is disassembling my dad's roses to make rose petal perfume. A couple of handfuls of rose petals, a cup of water, a squirt of washing up liquid and *voilà* – perfume. Chanel should have snapped me up while they had the chance. What was so great about that memory was the fact that my dad didn't 'throw a wobbly' at the sorry sight of his roses, but chose to enjoy the moment with me. He operated in Graciousness (the 'G' word). This is about being generous-hearted with forgiveness (yes, even with kids!).

Let's face it, our little angels can be irritating. So can their friends, and especially their friends' parents. Children can also have a real knack of spoiling our plans. Without graciousness in a household, minor annoyances can smoulder into resentments. Over time, resentments cut deep and hearts get broken. No wonder experienced mums put 'graciousness' in their top four essentials for a family foundation. This, therefore, is our second highly cherished pearl of wisdom that kick-starts even the most world-weary parent's 'va-va-voom'. It is a wonderful parent in a child's eyes who can be kind, rather than hard-hearted. Especially if they are justified for being grumpy!

I'm writing this book in the corner of my local Starbucks when my kids are in bed. OK, so Starbucks has great strawberry and cream Frappucinos, and I get to act like a real grown-up for a few hours a week. In the world of Starbucks, it seems there are two types of parents when it comes to the inevitable spilling of the child's milkshake everywhere. Regardless of the lightning speed the staff do the perfect mop-up, the response of the parent is often seriously irritated. Graciousness rarely gets a look in.

It makes me wonder if we 21st century parents are so uptight in not giving ourselves a break, that we don't give our own dearly loved kids a break for a genuine mistake. Every time I watch the kid spilling scenario I swear to myself that I will be gracious to my own kids. Why is it that kindness seems to have dropped out of fashion? Maybe it's time that it was reclaimed as something worth having in our fast-paced world. If I consider myself 'work in progress', surely I can extend the same to my kids for a genuine mistake. This is not about avoiding discipline, it's about cutting myself and others slack on the trek of life. Operating in graciousness – the 'G' word – is like adding fairy dust to your relationships. True happiness is simply not available without it.

Wisdom pearl number 3: Who calls the shots?

Now here's a crazy thing. How is it we can spot our kids are tired just by the way they hold their fork, yet we'd walk around like zombies for weeks before even considering slowing the pace a little? Why do many of us spend more money on the kids than we ever would on ourselves? Is it down to the kids where to go at the weekend? Sure, there is nothing on earth to rival stroking their downy heads as they sleep, sharing a 'wow' moment as they find a frog. But if our kids are the 'kingpins' in a household, we're storing up trouble. One of the consequences of a kid-led household is that mum is simply burned out like a twisty pretzel from relentless demands.

Most of the 'get a life' books aimed at parents seem to present 'getting a break from the relentless kids' as the ultimate goal. Take up t'ai chi, pottery, orienteering – ANYTHING to join the 'real world' and momentarily escape from the relentless demands of mommyland. I actually reckon our culture's obsession with getting 'space' from our kids might just not be doing our families any favours. First base in living life to the full is not actually about distancing ourselves from our kids or subconsciously categorising the kids as the 'competition' to getting our groove back. Sure, indulging in a spot of watercolour is not easy if your boys are doing the 'kid slippers' thing on your feet as your toddler tries to unbutton your shirt for a quick top-up. What's actually needed is to clamp down on the relentless demands, restore the right kid-parent power balance in a house. Without discipline, parenting simply has no 'va-va-voom'. Boundaries are crucial in building that solid family foundation; we haven't a hope without them. Discipline definitely deserves its place in our top four pearls of wisdom.

The word 'discipline' is peppered through parenting manuals and leaflets like suds in a bubble bath. Yawn. Naughty stair. Yawn, yawn. Boundaries. Yawn, heard it all before. Sure, discipline is the top thing for dealing with tantrums, sibling relationship meltdown, and mouldy cheese sandwiches under the bed. I'm on the frontline with all moms who care about raising a reasonably balanced kid not on the fast track to juvenile detention centre. Well, here's a bonus about discipline that's not so obvious, yet experienced mums have discovered. The goal of discipline is not just about raising a kid who is going to behave well at school, with siblings and at bedtime. Having boundaries, consequences and expectations is a definite first base to raising kids who are tooled up for a decent future. It's all too easy to give our children power and freedom when they need leadership and limits. If kids call the shots, it's time to wonder what a generation of self-centred deal-breakers we are breeding.

For more on boundaries and discipline see Chapter 2: 'This isn't the kid I ordered!'

Wisdom pearl number 4: Touching base with the little carpet-biters

The thought of a family life that is more dazzle than frazzle, more cherished than tedious, more real than autopilot... it's a glossy pearl that I just HAVE to take out of the parenting treasure chest. This precious pearl is about making it an absolute priority to connect with our kids each day. This is an easy one to miss in the busyness of life. Communication between parent and child is the glue that holds them together. Good communication gives a child confidence, security, a sense of identity. All it takes to connect is to share a joke, have a hug, read a story, kick a ball around. Something for the sheer pleasure of living. While a child may be surrounded by the incessant chatter of other children all day, this is no replacement for family interaction. Communication is the ultimate team builder. While we would all agree with this, the sheer pace of life can suck potential family time clean away. Time to haul some time back! Eating together is the old favourite for this, and there's no doubt that it's one of the best 'touch base' opportunities there are.

From one parent to another...

Lunch can be a hunt and gather affair. The dining room and kitchen are bustling with children eating, others seeking, others being served. The volume of people, sound and movement might just overwhelm an observer. To the practised ear, rather the tuned in ear, it is music. If put in words it might go something like this:

> Doors and drawers, slam and banging.
> Faucets and jugs pour and dripping.
> Silverware chimes, spills splatter,
> plates and bowls, rattle and clatter.
> Chomping and sipping, voices clash.
> The dishwasher door shuts with a crash.
> Above it all, a melody of conversation,
> So much to share without hesitation.

I have heard of homes that have silent meals. How can that be? I personally would be driven over the nearest cliff by the sound of chewing alone. A meal is the perfect time to regroup. Yes, we are together everyday but we all have different things going on in our lives. Ideally the picture would be of the Waltons gathered around the table but the reality is a little more elevated and animated. Around a table full of people, there can be a great deal of shouting to be heard with so many different conversations. Lunch it is more a time to mingle and connect face to face. It is a great time to talk, a great time to share!

In all this we add something more. Music is almost always playing in my house. At any given moment we break out singing when a familiar tune reaches us. My oldest daughter is in charge of kitchen clean up. She loves to sing while cleaning. Being fairly insecure about her voice, you would think she would look to see if the repairman was still there before breaking forth loudly with bravado, hands raised: 'Someday my prince will come!' Now that is a time to remember!

Then there is the dancing! I have more than one child who likes to pirouette and leap spontaneously. Just ask the shocked visitor who happened to be standing by the door when my daughter came bounding in. She realised he was in her landing zone while in mid air. It is still a mystery how she did not land in his arms. We suspect a miraculous development of air brakes. Many hours of joyful discussion have followed. Was his smile shocked or amused? A wonderful time to laugh!

Memories of stories, habits and jokes that no one else knows. If told, no one would understand. A collection of: 'You had to be there' moments in time. There will always be interruptions from the roaring world always offering and demanding to take our time. Time needs to be treasured, measured,

guarded, shared and given. Something so valuable is worthy of great care in how we use it.

www.homeschoolblogger.com/emmaus

When all is said and done...

Juggling like a lunatic does not have to be part and parcel of parenting in the 21st century. While becoming a domestic goddess and master of organisation can certainly ease that sense of incessant activity, it certainly is not the answer to raising great kids. It's all too easy to trade our 'mummy' role, for 'manager', and run the risk of losing closeness with our kids.

The very first steps in escaping juggling mania AND raising great kids are not half as complex as we might imagine. These are the precious gems of wisdom commended to you my mums the world over: Operate in graciousness, resist the urge to nag, gripe and hold grudges. Build the right 'power balance' in a household (i.e. the kids don't call the shots!). Finally, connect with each of your children, each day. The foundation of a great family gets built brick by brick, day by day. Even on the days when it feels like everything you built just came tumbling down, don't give up on the adventure. Your family is worth it.

2

This isn't the kid I ordered!

Usually by the time your in-house rascals can scale your wardrobe, the reality dawns that kids don't always turn out quite as you expected them to. Those mummy-tinted glasses keep getting knocked off, and you see your kid's flaws in glorious technicolour. Facing the reality that your little cherub is not actually made of fairy dust, tinsel and baby powder can be quite a wake-up call. Let's have a look at the three traps that are so easy to fall into should challenging kids become an issue in your house.

Trap 1: Just 'getting through' each day

Near our home, the local cattery had a revamp and was named 'pet hotel'. These lucky cats get meals delivered to their 'quarters', regular gentle walks, and optional extras such as shampoo, extra blankets and catty chews before bed. I speed past this resort about four times a day en route to my kids' various activities, usually with manic kids' music on full blast and the kids welding raisins into the upholstery to pass the time. On one particularly frantic excursion when I'd had to make a detour to recover a shoe 'dropped' out of the window, I paused by the traffic lights and gazed longingly at the pet hotel. If only I could check myself in, order shampoo and extra blankets, with nothing to disturb me for a couple of weeks other than a spot of gentle exercise and delivery of a few well-earned treats.

Sometimes, when my kids are pushing the limits, I find myself 'mentally' checking into pet hotel and blanking out the tough stuff. Anything to just get through the day. Everyone has times like this. However, going through day after day on this kind of autopilot is a serious demoraliser. Sure, we may be 'coping', but at what cost to our self-esteem and relationships? Mindlessly chugging through life has the effect of letting sense of purpose and control slip away. Regardless of how the children are behaving, all parents need a sense of direction and purpose in their parenting. This gives us the focus not to slip into ruts, or to live constantly in 'just getting through the day' mode. What would you like life to be like a month from now, a year from now? How would you like to see your family at these milestones? What are the exact behaviours that you would like developed within the house? What things could you initiate to make these a reality? Even a simple thing such as setting a few small daily goals can be enough to haul a parent out of autopilot and into a better quality of life.

If 'auto-pilot living' is a daily reality for you, it might be worth taking a long hard look at how much energy you have left for your kids once the rest of your life has taken its quota. If your kids are only ever getting the last dregs of your energy and passion, things need to change. I'm not being harsh, just keeping it real. If we love our kids with our hearts, let's love them with our time and energy too.

Trap 2: Giving the rebellious child some 'space' to come round

Crawling across the burning sands of early parenthood, it's that inbuilt love for this wriggling individual that keeps us just about hanging in there. A few years down the line, should they appear to throw it all back in your face, it can really hurt. This nagging sense of dissatisfaction with family life causes some parents to distance themselves emotionally from their kids. This is nothing to do with kids stretching their wings; it's an adult coping mechanism. Sure, kids need 'space' in the day to get on with their own interests. But they don't need emotional distance when they are knee-deep in a rebellious behaviour pattern. I've counselled parents who gave their rebellious child 'space', and were distraught to find the problems got worse. Rarely does a child work through a behavioural issue without positive input from someone who loves him. What is needed is re-establishment of unconditional love and re-establishment of boundaries. Connecting more, not less. How to make all this a reality in the crazy business of everyday life is the second part of this chapter. Before we dive into this, check out the third common trap that many of us fall into when it comes to challenging kids...

Trap 3: Softening the bumps of life

When kids start pushing the boundaries, another temptation is to juggle like a lunatic to provide safe, yet challenging, distractions for their energy. None of us set out to be controlling; we just want the best for the angels that we know they really are. This style of parenting can creep up on even the most well-rounded parent. Almost without realising you start polishing away, giving them a leg-up, and softening the consequences of their behaviour. We give them power and choices, when they really need leadership and limits.

The main problem with this style of parenting is that the opportunity for a child to learn about choices and consequences is simply missed out of the loop. These kind parents rarely realise this is going on, pouring themselves out selflessly to give their children the best start in life. Their gift is precious, yet what is also needed is the chance for the child to take on some responsibility for their own choices. When this is put into action, a whole cargo of skills develop, such as decision making and self-discipline. These skills, according to psychologists, are in the top five skills for a rounded and successful life. If something's in the top five, it's got to be worth having!

Not one to dish out advice that I can't take, I decided to do some research. OK, so I don't have an army of willing participants or a staff of keen boffins on hand. But I do have three unsuspecting victims (my trio) and a large dose of my own curiosity to see what happens if I ease off on the control freak pedal and let them learn consequences of their actions without me softening the blow. So when my unsuspecting daughter decided that she didn't WANT to put her shoes on to walk across the road with me to collect our keys from a neighbour across the road, I resisted the urge to duct-tape her flip-flops to her feet, give her a 30-minute lecture on podiatry and drag her kicking and screaming to collect the keys. Instead I nonchalantly replied 'OK' (without even a flicker of a grimace), and headed to the door expecting her to follow. Which she did with her independent little eyes sparkling, flashing a victorious look to her brothers. Sure, I confess I visually swept the road for any glass, sharp stones, snail shells and strode out with her, ignoring her whines as the hot tarmac stung her toes. I think I ought to pause here, dear reader, before you report me with stories of dragging a pitiful child across a busy freeway. The road is narrow, smooth and barely used. Anyway, we returned home with the keys and nothing more was said. Needless to say, she has not objected to 'out of house' footwear ever since. Sure, this was a tiny issue, but baby steps suit me just fine. Day-to-day issues are great for learning the real-world reality that choices have consequences.

That's three possible traps we could fall into when challenging children are on the rampage. Now, how about some positive inspiration to redress the balance...

How to have well-behaved kids

Over the last two years I have scoured the world and its experts for the best way to raise grounded kids. What I was after was answers for parents with kids who chuck their shoes out of the car, and have sussed that the game you've suddenly announced would be fun is actually from your 'self-esteem games for kids' book. Answers for 21st century parents who want to make the absolute best of their parenting adventure.

I guess you've already picked up my aversion to 'itinerary living', treating our families like projects to be organised. Nevertheless, some things, like having well-behaved kids, call for pulling out all the stops. This is not the time for muddling along, or filling the schedule so full with other activities we barely speak to our kids, other than to bark out the usual 'extract the nailbrush from the toilet' kind of orders. There are seven bases to cover if the home run we're after is a grounded, well-behaved kid.

Base 1: 'Nuggetty' love

'Nuggetty' love is about cherishing kids regardless of how things are turning out. Remaining bowled over by the child, even if we hate the attitude. For a parent, racked with frustration at her wayward child, it can be hard to see out of the difficulties. The kid's attitudes swamp everything else. Perhaps the hard bit of 'nuggetty' love is to love them actively and passionately, even if this appears to have no impact on their behaviour whatsoever. The goal of true 'nuggetty' love is not to gain back credits of good behaviour; the goal is to love because you love them. That's it. This kind of love may require us to swallow hard, and not be a nag. It's a choice whether or not to operate in 'nuggetty' love in a household. We choose whether to forgive, or hold a grudge. We choose whether or not to focus on faults, on a day-to-day basis. We choose whether to mentally check into 'pet hotel', or to actively cherish our kids. Tough choices for a burnt-out parent. Sometimes we can be so busy trying to 'fix' our kids that we don't get around to loving them in the midst of their struggles.

I'm not saying that discipline and correction of wrong behaviour isn't necessary; of course it is. But if that discipline is not founded on unconditional love, it's just like throwing seeds onto dry soil. None of us is perfect, so without unconditional love we are all forever striving to be 'good enough' to be cherished by someone. That's an empty way to live, and I so don't want to set up that pattern for my family. Nuggets of unconditional love are what make the hardcore foundation of a grounded kid.

Base 2: The habit strategy

The age-old strategy that has stood many a parent in good stead is 'plant a seed, reap a habit, pursue a habit, and reap a destiny' (Charlotte Mason). So my guess is building positive habits in my kids is the way to go. A negative habit that my kids slipped into a while ago was 'discontent'. You know, that attitude that is never satisfied, commenting how others have more, always pushing the boundaries? Well, I decided that sowing some 'content' habits in our household would make a world of difference for us. My husband and I sat our kids around the dining room table and said that as of that date 'discontent' or whinging/demanding behaviour was completely unacceptable and would immediately result in severe removal of privileges. Stunned silence followed; they mercilessly munched their hot dogs, flashing grimaces at each other. Even Dexter the hamster paused on his wheel with a 'What did *I* do?' look on his face. A week later, after removal of skateboards, and denial of permission to see a friend, the message was starting to hit home. I even went as far as writing 'NWZ' on a piece of paper (No Whinging Zone) and I'd flash it in a whinging child's face as a ten-second warning before their prized lightsabre would be stashed on top of the fridge. Reading this, it sounds rather neurotic, I know. Nevertheless, 'good habit sowing' really works, as many parents have discovered. The key is to stick with it, until new patterns become the family norm.

Great habits to include in your habit-building strategy could include: truthfulness, team work, generosity, diligence, respectfulness, graciousness, tidiness, forgiveness, initiative, thankfulness, patience, self-control. I'm sure you can think of more. These habits are great for all of us to take on board, not just the kids.

The top tips for good-habit sowing are:

- **Pick one habit at a time.**
- **Stick with it.**
- **Affirm a child as she develops the characteristic so that she sees herself as a patient/honest/ generous person. These positive labels will last a lifetime.**

Sure, words like 'diligence' may seem like they are out of a dusty 1960s manual on child-rearing. We have a dusty 1965 volume that features a bouffant 'ever-smiling' mother in a pretty apron, and a moustache-sporting father. The shape of the family now is much more diverse; life is different in so many ways. Nevertheless, these 'traditional' characteristics such as respect and diligence are real dazzling gems for positive 21st century family life. They are love in action, and the glue that holds families together. Simply too good to miss!

Note to self: Raising amazing kids doesn't just happen.

Building good habits into the family infrastructure is how to get there, one sparkly brick at a time.

Base 3: The 'B' word – making it work for you

Worked out what the 'B' word is yet? Well there's one 'B' word with real clout that really nails things: 'Boundaries'. Now before you skip over to the next section, stick with me just a minute. There might be a few swift moves in the realms of boundaries that have slipped your notice...

The 'Boundaries' master class

Boundaries are clear limits about what is acceptable, and what is not acceptable. They add structure and meaning to a world that pulls our kids in so many directions. Countless studies have shown how well children turn out with firm boundaries, and how poorly they turn out without boundaries being kept. Now here's the tricky bit: There is a huge difference between head nodding and thoroughly agreeing with the value of boundaries, and successfully making them happen at home.

I remember a crazy day when I realised that I hadn't defrosted the chicken, and the in-laws were arriving any second. The kids were running around the house like tornadoes and my husband wasn't due back for hours. I was stressed, frazzled and at the end of my tether. Then, my eldest called from the lounge, 'Can I have a quick play on the X Box?'(This was the very same X Box that I had just barred him from for a week for misbehaviour.) 'OK!' I shrieked, hacking away at the frozen chicken like a lunatic. Anything for a bit of peace! The next morning, I

found my youngest using a few Cheerios to fill her
jewellery box with 'rings'. Incensed by the extortionate
cost of chocolate-coated cereal, I blew an absolute
gasket. I dished out discipline for the small
misdemeanour (Cheerios), and yet failed to enforce a
boundary for something that actually mattered
(following through on the established boundary of 'no X
Box'). This is an example of how NOT to do boundaries!
The key with operating in successful boundaries, like
everything in the quest to escape juggle mania, is to keep
your word and be consistent. Boundaries mean
NOTHING if they are put aside during a busy day.
Successful boundary-setting needs to be clear, achievable
and consistent. Kids truly flourish when they know what
the limits and expectations are.

Base 4: Roast chicken revelations

It amazes me how much my kids nail me down to 'plan'
for the week ahead. OK, you could say it's just to ensure
they get equal 'allotted' skate park time and they can hold
me to that Toys4kidz visit that I put in the plan a week
ago (grrrrrrr). Nevertheless, I've noticed that routine
gives kids a handle on their world and minimises bad
attitude. Routines and family traditions give a great
sense of security in our crazy, ready-meal world. They
build memories, a sense of belonging and family. Even
something simple like a 'treat' family meal a week can
build security. Rooting a family together certainly makes
rebellion a less attractive option for a child. Some
parents are not keen at the thought of being tied to a

routine, as it seems to threaten their chances of a relaxing weekend. I guess I've been that way inclined. Well, take it from me: family routine is a delicious thing. There's happy juice to be had for all the family!

Base 5: What kids hear (gulp)

Well now, here's a surprising nugget that is a real maker or breaker on how kids behave: the stuff they hear their parents say. Good or bad comments that just rolled off the tongue somehow wedge in a kid's heart. Our tongues are such tiny wriggly bits of us – yet what power they have! Now I've realised the power of words, I try and master my words each day. The biggest shift I noticed when I became more aware of what I said was the reduction in sibling bickering. How's that for a bonus! Now, when bickering occurs I try and deal with that particular incident without generalising. I'm trying to rein in my comments about others, and I've shifted my focus. I remind them of great family outings, the moment they first met. I talk as if I believe the brother and sisters are utterly devoted to each other. Please don't imagine I'm in this rosy little world where by the wave of a verbal wand everything suddenly becomes picture perfect. I'm more of a Bridget Jones than 1960s supermother, and my kids can slam doors as well as the rest. Nevertheless, ditching the griping really does make a huge difference.

Base 6: Raising passionate kids

My kids' Bible story book has Goliath, a hairy, armour-clad Mr Incredible, facing a pale puny David with his knees knocking. Goliath has to be at least ten times David's height. A touch of artistic licence going on here, I think. But haven't we all felt as if our battles in life – our 'Goliaths' are at least ten times as tall as us, towering over us as we shiver in our boots? Well, puny David defeated his Goliath not by mighty skill, tools or trickery. He defeated him by holding onto what was true, right. His belief and passion were unshakable. I reckon a golden, diamond-encrusted key to raising grounded kids is to nurture their belief, and a passion for what is right and true.

Much of our society is engrossed in living for the moment, surviving the moment, or squeezing the most out of the moment. The key to raising families who are not consumed by this is to look at the bigger picture of life. What matters in the world? What matters in your country, your community? Caring about the bigger picture will undergird your child with a strength and purpose. Many children have an instinctive pull to world issues, be it climate change, or an orphanage they saw on CNN. Sure, tear-jerking songs that lament 'children are the future' can get tiresome. Nevertheless, these words are true; children *are* the future of our world. Let's raise them to care about the bigger picture.

Base 7: Kids are like set yoghurt

Skimming through books on the topic of raising children, you often come across the phrase 'children are like wet cement'. This phrase is used to remind us that attitudes and words around a child will stick with them for a lifetime. For sure, words, body language, even tone, impact a child's developing sense of themselves. After all, they perceive their value by our actions and attitudes. Now I'll pause here, just in case you feel like me when reading about how parents can wreck a child's self-esteem without even realising it. As if the responsibility of feeding, clothing, raising these challenging individuals wasn't full on enough! Now their future happiness, ability to function in the adult world are entirely dependent on our parenting! Someone book me into the pet hotel NOW!!! Sometimes, getting parenting right can seem an impossible task, like paddling upstream through treacle.

Yes, we can impact our kids' self-esteem for good and bad. Yes, the parent-child relationship is one of the most significant there is in their world. However, these little individuals are so much more than mirrors of our mistakes. When my youngest pokes her finger into a tub of smooth set yoghurt, it leaves a little dent in the yoghurt. Yet, after a while, the yoghurt 'gloops' back into place. Day-to-day parenting mistakes do have an effect, but you get another shot to learn from them and get it right the next time. I like to remember this when I see the 'kids are like wet cement' phrase. Indeed, they are on a path to adulthood and our parenting window is not open forever. Nevertheless, they are not heading for ruined lives should we not achieve perfect parent status 24/7.

When all is said and done...

If you read my last book you'll know that I'm a softie at heart who, under the influence of pregnancy hormones, cries at anything from fluffy bunnies in advertisements, to when Captain Kirk died in *Star Trek* (and I don't even LIKE *Star Trek*). But as each day goes by, I'm realising that loving cuddles on the 'good days' only go so far.

So, how do we prevent a child going off the rails? First port of call is that rugged, robust and secure thing called unconditional love. This is the best foundation there is. Loving kids in the midst of their struggles is key, not withholding affection until they behave. Then, step by step, start building good habits into the family infrastructure and start dealing with negative habits such as discontent. Now here's the tricky bit: being consistent with boundaries! This is the key to kids building their own stash of self-discipline and responsibility. Tempting as it is to mentally opt into 'pet hotel' when the going gets tough, actually taking hold of positive goals is a better option. Another great step is to establish family routines and traditions, start getting things in order. Finally, let's not forget that perfection is not the aim of parenting! All of this advice is tried and tested stuff, best put into action one little step at a time. Train a child well, with a few generous hunks of 'nuggetty' love, and one day they will soar like eagles.

From one parent to another...

How much further? Ah, those universal questions. They cross the lips of every child who travels by car, train, bus, plane, rickshaw, canoe or camel.

Last night, being of a somewhat philosophical bent (sometimes the rain does that to me) I was pondering the analogy of parenting as a journey. Sometimes it seems that it will never end... and where are we going, anyway? On days when the trip seems interminable... start looking for mile markers. You will be amazed and encouraged. At least I was!

We have four kids, each two years apart.

A BIG milestone came when I could run out for fifteen minutes alone and safely leave them at home. I was known to zip to the grocery store four times a day back then, giddy with newfound freedom. How well I remember the surreal pleasure of strolling around the store ALONE! The perfect peace... no squabbling siblings hanging off the sides of the cart and poking holes in the bag of frozen peas, while old ladies with blue hair and lipstick on their teeth warbled sentiments like 'These are the best years of your life, honey.' (WHAT!! You mean it's all downhill from here?)

Last night I noticed another milestone. As we sat down to eat dinner I realized that since our son grilled the pork chops, oldest daughter emptied the dishwasher, middle daughter peeled the carrots, and youngest daughter set the table, EVERYONE had contributed to the meal, without specifically being asked. It almost brought me to tears! Our children are turning into people... NICE people that I like... in spite of our parenting failures.

Next year our son can legally drive. I see another milestone looming, along with skyrocketing insurance premiums.

So parenting really is a journey. Are we there yet? Not even close. I'm not even sure where 'There' is anymore. But with each vista and valley, bumpy lane and hair pin turn we are making progress. I've resolved to notice the mile markers as we pass them; enjoy them, celebrate them, and remember them.

Yes, we have maps for this journey. Sometimes we don't follow them, or we try to take shortcuts. Sometimes there's a coffee stain covering the spot we need, so we have to muddle through the best we can. But let's enjoy the road trip. Let's roll the windows down and get our hair messed up, let's sing along with the music, eat cookies and leave crumbs on the upholstery!

I suspect the blue haired ladies are right. When we finally park the minivan at the end of this journey... we just may wish we were back on the road.

Eleanor Joyce, www.homeschoolblogger.com/ejoyce,ink

3
Ditching your baggage

Climbing the Everest of steps up to the snow sport centre, I realised that I'd taken the advice to bring changes of clothes a little too seriously. As my kids jousted with ski sticks, I huffed and puffed like a polar bear on heat trying to carry two bags of spare clothes. Chances of my husband being my shining sherpa in a padded jacket were melting fast as he cooed over a shiny beast of a snowmobile. As much as I would have liked to scamper around like a snow elf with the kids, I just couldn't. The bags were just too heavy, 'humph!' This chapter is about ditching the baggage that weighs us down (and I'm not talking bags of sweaters). Time to ditch the stuff that stops us living life to the full and leaves us juggling like maniacs just to keep afloat.

> *Oh, the worst of all tragedies is not to die young, but to live until I am 75 and yet not ever truly have lived.*
>
> Martin Luther King Jr

The baggage story

We go through life collecting mindsets, beliefs, experiences and emotions. Some of these serve us well on our life adventure, and some are toxic and drain us dry. Take, for example, Tallulah. At 17 years old she gets dumped by her boyfriend and picks up a small bag called 'rejected' that she carries around with her for a number of years. As the years roll by, a few more friends let her down and her neat little bag is now bulging a bit. Before long, 'rejected' has become a hefty bit of baggage to lug around. But she's a chick who likes to live her dreams so she throws it over her shoulder and gets on with life, swapping hands when it gets too heavy. She gets married, has kids and has a career shift. Within a few years she picks up a briefcase labelled 'disillusioned'. Life races on, and she picks up a snazzy little purse labelled 'past her prime' and a matching purse called 'can't control her temper' . Every day she dresses, does her hair and loads up all her baggage and goes for life. She's getting wearier by the day (not that she realises). At night she hops into her bed next to her husband, tucking the baggage in between them. They're all there – 'rejection', 'disillusionment', 'past her prime', 'temper'. Next day she heads off to the gym; maybe then life just won't feel so weighed down, so sluggish.

Life sometimes really sucks. Stuff happens and leaves us with baggage that drags us down. Now here's the bottom line: We can't take responsibility for others' actions to us, but we can take responsibility for our own lives. Resentment and disillusionment can fester in families, gnawing away day after day. We can choose to lay aside the weight and not accept that bag any more. I'm sure there are many church pastors, support organisations and friends who may help us on this journey. Nevertheless, choosing to take responsibility for our own life comes from our heart alone. Baggage ditching resets the gauge in your life and enables you to see more clearly about choices that may need to be made. Just because someone dishes a comment out doesn't mean it has to be accepted. If we don't ditch the baggage now it will be there, strangling joy, for the rest of our days.

Ditching the fake

Growing up, I had high hopes for me. You know, the usual... to be popular, successful loved, beautiful. How other people rated me I don't know, but I do know for sure that I was sometimes a harsh judge of myself. So, as if to fill the gap between who I actually was and who I wanted to be, I sometimes talked and acted to cover up the gap. Indeed, there is no greater juggler on the planet than the one who is busy in the business of 'spin'. I'm not talking about the underhand monopolising that politicians become famed for, but spinning a picture that isn't quite the real person. A crucial part of living life to the full is to be honest and real about where you are at in life. Welcome the real person, the whole package, just as you are. Sure, there are magic diets, detox systems, extreme makeovers promising to transform your life. The problem is, these quick fixes only address the surface of a person. Deep inside is the real person, where the true beauty lies. This is the place to be honest about where you are at, and initiate change based on self-loving rather than self-dissatisfaction.

Ditching your man?

'Oh, so it's one of THOSE books', I hear you mutter. One of those 'girls don't need guys' books that the bookstores are bursting with. Well, actually no. The chaps do have the monopoly on socks on the floor and not always saying the right thing just when we need it. Guys, like girls, can sometimes get things very wrong. Before we start, let me ask you a question:

What things you would like to change about your man?

Now, can you think of some things that you would like to change about yourself?

Which question resulted in a bigger list of things? Am I right in guessing your list of things HE needs to change is far lengthier than the list you gave yourself? You see, I've noticed that we girls have a real tendency to notice our guy's weaknesses before our own. It's easy to let a nugget of resentment sit there gnawing away at your relationship. I have a couple of pearls of wisdom from one friend to another if you've ever resented your man for your juggling mania.

To me, being married is a messy, magical affair. Just like having kids, it doesn't work out in reality like we expect. Let me tell you about the day that I was stuffing more into the tumble drier than is humanly possible. I was grumbling away in my head about a husband who didn't act how I wanted, didn't say what I wanted him to say. I sounded like the women you hear discussing their men (or kids) at the school gates – having a real grumble.

It annoys me hearing other women go on like this, but it was different for me – I was JUSTIFIED. There I was, on my knees cramming the last swimming-pool-water-sodden towel into the drier, and something happened... I realised that I had a choice. I could either gripe about my very real gripes OR I could not gripe. I WANTED to continue grumbling; I was SO justified! If I didn't gripe he would never know what a sacrifice it was for me NOT to gripe and THAT would be doubly unfair! Then a still small voice reminded me – a few years earlier I had devoted my life to him; he was my husband.

These days, being a wife seems to have little more significance than being a vegetarian or deep sea diver. It's just something you do. It doesn't have to be this way; marriage could actually end up being the ultimate adventure, a journey so rich that our kids are inspired by the ride. I've realised that marriage is our window for true love. Every gripe is using up our window. So I did the thing that I've seen other couples with good marriages do (we're not talking matching tracksuits here): I made him number one in my life. Not number four, or twenty-five, but number one. Now if this is starting to sound a bit 'doting apple pie' for you, stick with me for just one more moment. Great marriages don't just happen; if we don't go all-out to build something great we will never get there. Want a fabulous marriage? Don't wait until your husband is perfect in every way until you devote your heart. This is perhaps the wisest piece of advice I was ever given, and now I share it with you.

Ditching obligation living

Here's how I see it. If invitations to parties/school fête preparations/strangers' weddings all had a little slip marked 'tick for either "yes" or "no"', life would be so much easier. It's almost impossible to get out of the invitations that go something like this: 'Which Saturday would suit you to come over for a cheese fondue?' Even if you're allergic to cheese, your host-to-be will wink as if you're just being coy. 'Not to worry, there'll be plenty of Derek's radish casserole to be had too.' Last year I was invited to an occasional friend's daughter's eighteenth birthday party. Now that would have been great if I was eighteen or even twenty-one. But to an eighteen-year-old, anyone over twenty five might as well be shuffling along in her tan tights to collect her pension. PLUS I like to think of myself as a young, 'with it' kind of chick. The sight of a darkened room heaving with bronzed teenage bodies, navel rings sparkling in the disco light, might just burst my bubble. So I declined, not with an honest 'I'd rather have leg vein surgery, thanks' but something more along the line of 'I'm so sorry, I'm already booked that day' (OK, so it was only a date with a Starbucks latte). My occasional friend was so shocked I'd said no, you'd think I'd just parked in her drive. There is so much pressure in our world to say a gleeful 'yes' to any invite or request thrown our way.

Much unnecessary juggling is due to people saying 'yes' to things they should have said 'no' to in the first place. It is wise to guard your time and energy, releasing it only when you are certain. Sure, there is a sense of satisfaction in being involved in lots of things, but it's not worth the effort if it leaves you burnt out. A sense of duty is what draws many of us to offer generous slices of our time and energy. This is based on what we perceive is the 'right thing to do' in a situation. Throughout history many women have been magnificent carers, friends, managers, leaders as they answered the call of duty. These have been women of integrity; their lives blessed many. For many, it cost them dearly. Duty, I believe, is only a noble response when it is based on the individual's conviction that taking on a role is absolutely right for them in that situation. Bowing to the pressure of other people's expectations is an entirely different thing. I encourage you to give generously with your time and energy, but not to be pressurised into it. Your time and energy are limited, and very precious.

Ditching the couch potato

The thing about inspiration, for whatever you do in life, is that it needs the headspace to be birthed and come out. Renée Zellweger was once asked how she lost her 'Bridget Jones weight' so quickly. She replied, 'I just run a lot. I don't do it for shape or health reasons; I do it because that's when I get the headspace to think properly.' I was inspired after reading this and slipped on my joggers and belted around the neighbourhood. I'm not saying I reached mental liberation (quite hard when you're puffing like a warthog yet trying to look sprightly every time you haul yourself past someone out washing their car). Yet, she's right, there's something very liberating about being just you, on a stretch of ground with the wind in your face. Now there's a good reason for powering down the laptop and getting some life-boosting exercise. Sure, it whips your body into shape; add to that the knowledge that your body is getting stronger by the day and you really feel truly alive.

Ditching last-minute juggling

Some people multi-task with such precision that EVERYTHING has to run to plan or they get uptight. Their stress is not so much losing their keys on a regular basis, but the stress of someone else hanging their keys on the wrong hook. Others are equally intent on juggling the world, and let details slip through the net on a quest for getting the big stuff done. Hence the keys get put in a different place every time they arrive home, guaranteeing next morning chaos.

Regardless of which type of multi-tasking you lean towards, have you noticed how we all seem to have an innate sense that things should have an order? I guess it's how the world works, the seasons, the cycles of life. Everything has its place, to the tiniest detail. Yet this order and place does not take away from the beauty and sheer magnificence of the world. The world has purpose, function and significance. Even the most insignificant weed has a growth cycle, seeds, flowers for pollination. The details matter. So, rather than go on about 'a place for everything, and everything in its place' (yawn), I like to take my inspiration from the utterly beautiful, exhilarating and indeed ordered natural world. Somehow that's far more inspiring. The answer to ditching last-minute panic? Well, we all know it's about thinking ahead, putting the details of our life in their proper place. The inclination to make this a reality when your life is bursting at the seams is the tricky bit.

Thinking of the details to be addressed in life as the petals on a flower, the colours on the rainbow, the palms on a palm tree... now that's inspiring. Taking care of the details completes an ordered picture and the real beauty of life can be enjoyed.

Ditching the juggling mindset

Just before Christmas last year I was the closest I'd ever been to a super-organised house. After a marathon of wrapping, cooking, blitzing, stuffing, shopping, I slumped dazed on the sofa. The Christmas tree twinkled and the kids scampered in the 'snow'. Well, it was actually thousands of white polystyrene balls they had just liberated in the garage. They were whooping with delight, covering the lawnmower and bikes with 'snow'. As the garage is officially not my territory, I opted to chill out in my exhausted bliss, rather than interrupt the snow carnage. When I find myself in an unexpected moment of peace, my usual reaction is to take a quick scout around for a job I could get ahead of the game on. Usually the floor is littered with Lego or pink feathery scarves, so I'm on my hands and knees like a maniac picking up before the world roars in on me again.

But this time, there was no Lego or kids' dressing-up clothes in sight, not even a half-eaten lollipop stuck down the side of the couch. So, ignoring the muffled whoops from the garage, I poured myself a glass of fine wine and decided now would be the perfect moment to relax. So I settled down with a good book. Well, almost. The phone rang and I answered it (mistake). It was only a short call, but en route back to the sofa I threw a quick load of washing into the machine, emptied the bin and had a quick urge to clean the inside of the microwave. I gave away my precious moment of peace, just like that. Regardless of how full (or not) a life is, a multi-tasker will always have the urge to find something to set to work on. The knack is to resist the urge sometimes. I guess it's a matter of seeing relaxation as a really precious commodity, rather than merely a pause between activities.

Ditching single-seat living

Due to the fact that I keep getting distracted by emails, I may not get this book finished until man is walking on Mars, no-chip nail varnish actually works, and buxom is the 'new black'. Most of us have a love/hate relationship with our email inbox: we hate hundreds of emails that overload and demand our time, yet somehow we still love that sweet 'bling' sound meaning a new email has just arrived. It's bizarre that we live in a world that communicates like never before, yet isolation is still the number one complaint. Billions of emails and texts whizzing around cyberspace each day, yet many feel alone. People who juggle busy lives can often feel lonely even when their life is stuffed full of people. Frantic parents, especially, can find themselves treating friendships as another item on the 'to do' list. Sometimes it takes a rethink to realise that other parents aren't merely objects associated with our kid's life.

In our 24/7 parenting world there are some pre-children realities that we all miss... Saturday morning 'lie-ins'; not having to speak in code; having a glass of red wine with a meal; NEVER having to go to Toys4kidz. Well, other than the arrival of our precious babies, there's one bit of life that actually has the potential to get much better when you have kids. Friends! Pre-children, millions of us wouldn't recognise our neighbours if we ran them over in their driveway. Even if your devoted mum lives nearby, no doubt you will have realised something crucial: Each generation has a different set of parenting rules. For example, our mothers crocheted orange blankets and wheeled us around in huge metal-wheeled prams. We have baby sleeping cocoons, and wouldn't know a crochet needle if we sat on one. We opt for three-wheeled off-road 'baby transport systems' suitable for any jungle terrain (well, you never know). We enrol toddlers in educationally enhancing activities, yet our mothers can't see why they can't just play in the garden with half a dozen cotton reels. Hence, friends in our generation are the ones who really 'get it' about what matters in our world.

Sure, you don't want to go giggling to Starbucks with just anyone who's got a pocket full of Barbie shoes and used tissues; but keep a look out as friends are the fairy dust of life. We all want great friends to cheer us on in our dreams. Someone to help pick up the pieces should we find ourselves sobbing into the shag pile after a hard day. To be a true friend involves putting some grudge busting into action, a dash of kindness, a generous dollop of honest talk, topped off with liberal opportunities for raucous laughter.

Note to self: Taking the time to connect with people, rather than give minimal attention, is often all it takes.

Here is an ode to my friends: Jo, Deborah and Danielle (ten kids between them). They are passionate about their path in life; they live for so much more than the moment.

They are real and honest, and genuinely care about the jellybean-hogging, over-excitable me. Who deserves an ode from you? Buy them a big bag of jellybeans! Friends like surprises. The fluffier, the better (just don't combine fluffy and jellybeans – phuffth!).

When all is said and done...

There are a number of negative mindsets which are baggage and weigh us down. Ditching these will transform your life. First thing to let go of – living to impress others rather than being who you are. Many mums are stuck in a rut of making out they are supermum when actually they are really struggling. Being real about where you are at means others can get close enough to join you on your journey. Many of us also get into a rut of taking on too much, as we are unable to refuse other people's requests. It is wise to guard your time and energy, releasing them only when you are certain. While many women have risen to the call of duty and have led rich, fulfilling lives, be wary of making life choices when you are under pressure from others. Building great friendships will certainly help give a sense of perspective and grounding should your world be in a spin. Lifelong relationships are key to riding the waves of parenting successfully. While marriage gets bad press, I would say that it actually has the potential to be your ultimate adventure, a journey so rich that your kids will be inspired. Just don't wait till your husband is perfect before you devote your heart! Finally, travel light – let grudges and others' comments slip through your fingers. Choose life!

4

How to turbo-boost your kid's self-esteem

First, breathe a long sigh of relief. You see, unlike what our guilt mojo might whisper to us, kids who aren't currently well-tooled up with high self-esteem are not automatically destined for failure and the therapist's chair. Kids have different temperaments, and some find it easier to grow in this area than others. Some will have to work harder to build great self-esteem, navigating their way through the hurdles of life. Self-esteem is one of those things that flavour every area of a person's life. Being informed, motivated parents on the issue of self-esteem is a HUGE benefit to our kids. The reality is that how your child's self-esteem develops will affect the pain or joy your family will have over the next twenty or thirty years. How daunting is that! If you're daunted with me, and yet also up for tooling yourself up in this crucial bit of parenting, read on...

'Kid – I believe in you'

When our kids think we believe in them, they grow to believe in themselves. When they get the message through our words or actions that we don't reckon they're capable of much, they'll live like they're not capable of much. So, the million-dollar question: Do you believe in your kid? I'm not asking if your kid is perfect, or if they're growing up how you expected, or if they're doing well in their schoolwork. That's not what it's about. It's about having faith that they have the potential to grow from strength to strength, to overcome and be great. This is one to consider, because your faith in them really is the crux of their self-esteem.

'Hey, kid – I believe in you' is the kind of line you hear in a Hollywood family movie. You know, the ones where the kid is about to hit the baseball that will win the match, that will rescue a neighbourhood from certain ruin. Kid grits his teeth, dad gives him the thumbs up from the sidelines, kid whacks ball sky-high and everyone leaps from their seats cheering and hugging each other. If only life was always like that! For some kids, the reality of life not always working out, despite their efforts, is enough of a justification to give up.

'See, I told you I couldn't do it!' This is the response that all parents hate to hear, and it seems to be the flip side of telling a kid, 'Go on, you can do it.' The key is to be consistent in your belief in them, even if their achievement level is disappointing. In the long term your faith in them WILL sink in, but you have to be committed to it for the long haul. If a kid appears to be failing frequently, it's always worth trying something that they have more of a chance of achieving in. Succeeding in small things will build them up, especially if their achievement is not in direct competition with your local super-achiever (I'm sure you know one!). One of the biggest ways to show that you believe in your kid is to take the time to connect with their world, answer their questions, show that their opinions matter.

From one parent to another...

At bedtime, the boys get to ask their Dad ANY question in the world. I love that in this way they are growing in knowledge, but they're also getting to know their Dad. They just came off of 'How do they make such-and-such?' questions, 'What if?' questions, and now they're into 'Who invented?' questions. This has my husband having to get back to them, often bringing an encyclopaedia up the next night, or performing an internet search together. We just got a periodic table for their wall to help out since using it so naturally comes up during some of these questions.

Past topics have been kites, bandicoots, machine guns, kinfolk, meaning of life, grey matter, foreign countries, ceiling fans, money, tallest buildings, where does the night go in the daytime, I could go on and on and on with such a wide variety of subjects!

I'm so excited about the relationship they are building with their Dad through this. Some questions are just about life issues, you never know. They've been doing this for over a year now. Lastly they read the Bible and say their 'I love yous' and give kisses...I love to peek or listen in!

Sandi, www.homeschoolblogger.com/Titus2Woman

The power of our words

'Mop Head' was my nickname when I was a kid. My aim had been to get my hair cut in a trendy layered style but somehow I ended up sporting a look that was very...mop-like. Now the thing with labels, be it nicknames or comments, they can stick. If they're not positive, they can wreak havoc with a kid's self esteem. OK, so we can't do a huge amount about the occasional snipe from popularity-crazed Kieran on the soccer field. We can, however, put a veto on adult comments that undermine our kid, even if they are said quite innocently. Well, let's just bounce them back!

'Is she a bit shy?'... 'Oh no, she's a great thinker.'

It's empowering when we replace old stereotypes with more positive labels. Instead of 'feisty', think 'assertive'. Instead of 'noisy', think 'sociable'. Instead of 'intense', think 'intelligent'. Just in case you've had a quick swig of latte and thought, 'Oh, it's one of THOSE books where everything is whitewashed with sparkly positives to make everyone feel better' – well, no. I'm the first in the queue dealing with bad habits that my kids pick up. However, having a positive spin on your kids is simply refusing to let stereotypes settle on them at such a young age. They ARE work in progress, and if their parents don't believe in them, who will?

Flattery is not encouragement. Cooing over everything your child does throughout the day will dilute the words and have no benefit. Praise has to be deserved. Kids know when they have earned praise and when they haven't; they can smell empty praise a mile away. Rather than gushing, 'You're SO great', it's better to be specific:

'I noticed how you kept your cool then. You're going from strength to strength as a big brother.' In the busyness of life it's so easy to miss the opportunities for genuine recognition. Be warned – miss them and they will certainly happen less and less. This isn't a time to be slow on the uptake; seize the moment for encouragement and give it all you've got!

Constructive discipline verses destructive discipline

Think 'baseball' in our family, currently, and you won't be thinking of cheering crowds and not a dry eye on the stand. You see, one of my little angels walloped one through a window recently, so 'baseball' is not a great word to drop into the conversation at the moment. It's at those 'blow your top' moments when your kids really wind you up that it is SO hard not to give them a negative label: 'Why don't you ever look what you're doing!'

All kids misbehave at one time or another; discipline is crucial in ensuring boundaries and limits. Here are a few tricks to turbo-boost constructive discipline, rather than destructive discipline.

Destructive: 'Stop grumbling! I don't know why I bothered bringing you.'

Constructive: 'Take a moment to yourself, then come and tell me what the problem is.'

The key part to this is separating the child's actions from the child itself. Self-awareness is such a handy tool for anyone to develop, especially in the teen years. Here's a teen who's growing in self-awareness:

Talking, talking and more talking by
Spunkyjunior (age 16)

I have a problem. It's not that big a deal... except I can't help but do it. I talk. And talk. And talk some more. Sometimes I talk too much. Now I know talking's not a problem, it's what we do (yeah I've tried emailing my mom when she's in the next room). Sometimes my talking gets the better of me.

My brother's friend has the same problem. The kid just can't stop talking. I was walking past him one day and he had his nose in a book. And he was still talking... non-stop to himself. (Just so you know... I'm not THAT bad). There are many times when I say things that are wrong. I tell my mom a bad thing my sister did to me. I say things that I really regretted saying afterwards. There's no way to take your words back. Once it's said, it's said (too bad we're not more like computers... you know it would be nice to have an undo button every once in a while). I'm learning there are times to talk, and times to keep my tongue quiet.

Kristin Braun, www.spunkyjunior.blogspot.com

How BIG is your child's world?

If kids grow up knowing that the world is their oyster and they have life ahead of them, they are more likely to put things into action to fulfil their dreams. If you genuinely expect your child to make good life choices, take a moment to smile. Your expectation will be inspirational to them.

Now I have noticed something about parents' expectation that is kind of the flip side of the positive, life-affirming expectation we've been talking about. This kind of expectation has a capital 'E' and it is plastered all over the schedules of the achievement-orientated parents who are driven to push their child to achieve, achieve, achieve. Even this morning as I dropped my son off at tennis lessons, I heard another mum grumbling to the coach about her son: 'He would achieve so much if he put his mind to it. He just hasn't got the get-up-and-go. It's the same at his golf lessons, swimming class, karate club, chess club and boy scouts.' With all those activities scheduled, I'm not surprised his get-up-and-go had got up and gone! Indeed, with a parent who publicly discussed his failings, no wonder this kid is operating on autopilot. You can tell when expectation and demand for achievement are the driving factor in a family, when the parents talk about their kids as if they are apprentices rather than kids.

Widening children's horizons is not about taking foreign holidays or enrolling them in expensive clubs. It's more about facilitating a wide variety of experiences for them – camping, fossil hunting, vegetable growing. A crucial part of learning how to be a good communicator is meeting people from varied walks of life. Sometimes a parent's life can be so busy that life just ticks along in the same groove, year after year. Widening horizons, even in a small way, is inspiring for adults and kids alike. Variety really is the spice of life.

Top tips for building self-esteem

- Don't assume that because you love them, they know you love them. Kids need love to be translated into words, hugs, kind actions, reliability, empathy, quality time, patience, interest... All that stuff is talking their love language. Kids aren't mind readers.

- Don't give them 75 percent of your attention all the time. Haul that 25 percent back from what distracted you and give it to your kid. Then, when you've finished, give 100 percent to the other item requiring your attention.

Tomato stake parenting

Sometimes the biggest barrier to nurturing a younger child's self-esteem is that they can't get out of the rut of their own misbehaviour. 'I'm trying to be good, but I just can't!' Tomato stake parenting is a great tool in training a kid to grow strong and straight:

From one parent to another...

Basically tomato stake parenting is about keeping young ones at the side of the parent throughout the day. Staking the tomato plants keeps them from drooping and spoiling the fruit. I realized that in the busyness of our house with two older boys and plenty of other responsibilities, I wasn't keeping my little one close enough to me. I decided to give tomato stake parenting a try...

It was hard getting used to keeping him closer to me most of the time. My children are spread apart in age so I had got spoiled to having more freedom as a mommy. While I was busy doing things around the house, my little guy could just about destroy the house or wander into the yard. He was fast and was not content to be held very often. He just wanted to be on the go. Unfortunately I often gave in, and then had to pay the price later because I had given him too much freedom.

I began requiring that he sit with me peacefully sometimes, even if it forced me to put aside what I was doing to train him how we expected him to behave. Other times it required me to sacrifice what I was doing to play with and monitor him. Many times I couldn't stand and talk to the other moms at gatherings because I needed to stay close to his side while he played with the other kids so I could make sure that he was behaving correctly.

Slowly the behaviour began to improve though, as well as his patience for dealing with times when things weren't going his way. Of course, my behaviour was also improving. I was learning to pay more attention to him and to focus on teaching him how to deal with the world around him. This little guy is more demanding at times than his two brothers were put together. Now I try to remember that visual of the tomato plants growing straighter and stronger with the proper staking and remind myself that I need to be that stake for my children so that they can grow straighter and stronger.

Nancy Carter, www.homeschoolblogger.com/tn3jcarter

Growing their own 'I can do it' nuggets

A powerful tool I've found is to discuss a goal with your child which is achievable and desirable for them. With one of my kids recently, this has been learning to swim. We sat down and discussed our goal (swimming) and then possible options for achieving it (swimming lessons or going swimming often as a family). He chose the family swim option. Hence my tumble drier now groans at the sight of another batch of sopping towels, and I'm convinced that my hair has a chlorine-green hue to it. Many a time I wished I was cosily watching him from the viewing gallery rather than up close through panda eyes. But I was right there, cheering along, as he swam his first width. I wouldn't have missed it for the world. I noticed that by letting him have a lead on how he reached his goal, he was empowered. It's so easy to be a bossy parent and not give our kids the opportunity to grow their own 'I can do it' nuggets.

How to obliterate 'stinkin' thinkin''

'Inner dialogue' is psychologist lingo for the inner chatter that goes on in our minds as we go about our day. My habit of muttering to myself occasionally is along the same lines, but rates far higher in the self-embarrassment stakes. OK, so now you know that I chat to the fish and I'm just one step away from shuffling down the sidewalk talking to lamp posts, I'll continue. 'Self-talk' is critical for how children shape their view of themselves. One of THE MOST POWERFUL ways to turbo-boost self-esteem is to be positive in your self-talk. That said, I've noticed that kids seem to easily slip into negative self-talk. Have you ever heard a kid mutter, 'I'm an idiot' after making a mistake? I rest my case. Most things in parenting take regular working on every day, to bring about change that will last a lifetime. Here we go in three life-changing steps:

1. Be a great example

Let your kid hear you giving yourself positive affirmations throughout the day. OK, if you're a muttering nutter like me, this'll come easy, but for the rest of you it may feel weird at first. Saying things like 'I'm really pleased how I reorganised the cupboard', 'I'm really pleased how I kept trying at my tennis; now I really enjoy it.' Hearing this makes it somehow acceptable for a child to start to think in an affirming way. This affirmation talk is not just a one-off; let it become part of normal life. (It feels kind of good too!)

2. Have a family 'I can' catchphrase

There are a few well-known ones that you can put your family's spin on, such as 'Try, try, and try again' . A simple phrase said in your own family's way can be good. I use 'The Bullivants always do a proper job!' We also use 'I can do all things through Christ who strengthens me!'

3. Lasso negative self-comments

When a negative comment slips out I pretend I'm swinging a lasso around my head, then chuck it in my kids' direction, loop up the comment, then go to the window and chuck it out. This one makes you look rather silly. My kids think I'm fruit-loopy doing this, but hey, I'm up for a giggle if you are. It's a great way of encouraging awareness of self-talk.

A winner's strategy

'It's a dog eat dog world. Only the tough will make it.

Donald Trump, billionaire

In the TV series *The Apprentice*, high-fliers compete to woo billionaire Donald Trump with their business acumen to win a dream job. It's one of those reality shows that is hard to resist – watching a bunch of business twenty-somethings use every trick in the book (and some that aren't) to show their business skills and beat their competitors. At the end of each show the 'weakest candidate' is fired and packed off home in a taxi away from the luxury Trump Tower in New York City. One thing I noticed about these 'failures' which showed why they were picked for the show in the first place: upon being fired, each talked only of what strengths they felt they brought to the table, and how Trump missed out on seeing their skills further. What struck me was this wasn't big talk to cover up their failure. All of these candidates, despite the crushing blow of being publicly rejected, did not swerve in their self-belief. THAT is the winner's strategy, not just in business, but in all chunks of life from sports to family life. 'Not giving up' is a great skill to learn.

A note on winning: For me, the aim of this section is not get pumped up about raising a future winner, wealthy and successful. Sure, this may happen; your turbocharged offspring may be a future Olympian, astronaut or president. However, the chasing of wealth and power will never satisfy, because there's always more to be had.

Here's an example of one kid, BJ, who grew to be a true winner:

From one parent to another...

In my mind's eye, I can still see the little boy who stood in the middle of the hospital lobby reciting poetry, with wide blue eyes and his little-boy lisp, to an adoring audience of elderly cancer patients. This little boy, my youngest son BJ, was as at home on the local cancer floor as he was in our living room, since I was helping care for my mother, who was dying of kidney cancer.

What a little trooper he was, never knowing from day to day whether we would be in our living room, the chemo lounge, Grandma's lovely home, or a hospital room. Each day he was surrounded by the very sick and dying. And each day he entertained them all with his reading and recitations. His grandmother's pain was relieved for a time as she sat there just being proud of this special little boy who was always at her side. She took such joy in introducing him and showing him off to everyone.

Even at the age of 7, BJ learned about life and death, compassion, kindness, joy in the midst of great sorrow, how to relate to those who are ill, and how to be there when someone needs you. He was the best medicine many of those patients had each day, for he made them think of better days and better times in their lives, and tapped into long forgotten memories. He brought them joy.

He was there as his grandmother passed from this world into heaven. He will always remember that he was the last person that she spoke to, and remember the special bond they had, because he was able to be there, through it all.

It seemed so fitting that these last two years of BJ's school age years are ending much as they began. As he gave up his dream of graduating early, he was helping his sister realize her dream of helping her baby survive a pregnancy fraught with problems. When she was admitted to the hospital for complete bedrest, he helped to run her business. He learned to run a business, to work harder than most adults, and the meaning of self-sacrificial love.

His niece Ellora was born and made it all worthwhile for 10 all-too-short days before her sudden, unexpected death. And BJ was there for his sister as she handed her child from her own arms into the arms of Jesus. This autumn finds my son busy planning on how to keep his 82-year-old grandfather (who was diagnosed with lung cancer), busy through the autumn this year. He plans to take him deer hunting as they have done every year, and to make sure that they both continue playing on the dartball team. Grandpa is the most important person in his life, and I know that BJ will be there through it all for him, as he has been for so many others.

You might ask if his childhood has suffered. Perhaps, in the traditional sense. But in the areas that will help him succeed in life, he is far ahead of his peers. BJ has proven himself a leader and a doer. He knows what it is to live life to the full.

Kathy Kin, www.homeschoolblogger.com/iluvtheland

Mistakes – the real deal

Messing up in life is hard. The thing is about making mistakes, we still have a choice: to walk into the same mistake again or to pick ourselves up, turn around and not do it again. Learn from it. Remember, I'm no 'made it' parenting author with picture book, perfect kids. On the mistakes front, I've been there. I know what it is to be stuck in a rut that was bad for me. YET I also know that I don't have to continue in bad choices; I can choose differently, and I do. I am stronger and more alive now because I learned from my mistakes. I chose life. Now I don't want my kids to make big life mistakes, but I'd better be careful on this one. You see, if I give my kids the message that mistakes are toxic, I will deny them the opportunity to see mistakes as a chance to pick themselves up and persevere. This skill is as crucial to your kid as any one there is. Mistakes are a chance to start afresh and can be real, can be springboards to new things.

We're worth it too!

We've all had a kid act as if they were giving the best parent in the world a big hug and actually they were wiping their nose on your shirt. Having a nice, taut pre-children tummy morph into an appendage that almost buffs the floor really pulls the self-esteem rug from many a mum. I've not had many years of married life when my first thought and every breath haven't been somehow connected to my gaggle of kids. I've not had many years when I haven't had to keep an ear out for at least one of them posting toys into the nearest toilet cistern. Despite the fact that my kids don't usually put themselves in life threatening situations any more than once a day now, somehow my energy is still sucked out well before lunch and my self-esteem splutters. 'Boosting my kid's self-esteem? You have to be joking!' a friend of mine said as she came up for air between a toddler who tried to cut the cat's tail off and an eleven-year-old refusing to leave her room. 'My own-self esteem hasn't had a look in for years!' The thing about self esteem that's so burnt out it resembles a twisty pretzel, is that it IS retrievable. You've got to get the family balance right; treasure yourself as well as the kids. I guess the key is not to see our own needs as direct competition with the rest of the family's. It's all too easy to meet everybody else's needs but your own, and your self-esteem steadily leaks away.

Check out Chapter 6: 'For your eyes only', for a generous dollop of self-esteem boosting for parents (we're worth it too!).

When all is said and done...

Believing in your child, regardless of current achievement, is the crux of building their self-esteem. This may require the ditching of negative labels about their character, as these tend to stick for life. It's worth remembering that kids can smell empty praise a mile away; flattery will not build their self-esteem. Genuine encouragement is best given on the spot towards a specific characteristic or behaviour. Be warned – should we miss opportunities for genuine recognition, they will happen less and less. Unless you communicate that you're proud, your child may well assume that you're not!

Tomato stake parenting, keeping a child close

throughout the day, is a tried and tested way to redirect a child towards positive behaviour. The quiet, constant presence of an adult is a real security booster. Another booster is to eliminate 'stinkin' thinkin'' and to develop positive inner dialogue throughout the day. This is learned by example; we simply can't do this kind of hands-on parenting from a distance! When mistakes do come your child's way, encourage them to learn from it, and persevere. Some of the best self-esteem growth happens when a child overcomes a difficulty. When children value their uniqueness, they protect themselves from many of the dragons out there: drugs, alcohol, self-destruction, making poor choices.

5

Rebooting your kid's imagination

Life can sometimes feel like it is little more than a collection of 'must dos' and 'don't forgets'. Vacuuming the dog, extracting the hairbrush from the toilet, and other such essentials can eat up time so all else goes on the back burner. The thought of inspiring a kid's imagination is wonderful, yet somehow life often gets in the way. I've been really challenged by this, as I want our home to be so much more than a pit stop. I want it to be bursting at the seams with challenge, adventure and inspiration. Intrigued? Here's where the challenge took me...

In the grip of the one-eyed monster

I think one of the biggest parenting issues for me right now is how much video games and TV are used as a replacement for kids generating their own entertainment. Let's face it; it's so much easier to let them while away a couple of hours on the latest console, than have them mincing around the kitchen, whining. The bottom line, however, is that too much TV/console/video game time 'fills up the imagination shelf' in kids' brains.

I remember very well the day I started to consider what my kids' TV/computer/console weekly hour count actually was. Now I wasn't quite *Inspector Gadget* skulking around with a notebook to record any family member touching a keyboard, but I did keep an eye on the hours swallowed up. I'm not going to tell you how many hours my kids actually clocked up, but it's fair to say I was mortified. And yes, I knocked five hours off the weekly total when chatting with my friends about it! So, before you could say 'Sonic the Hedgehog' we swiftly established a new boundary of a fixed 'screen time' each week (ours is six hours). It was up to the kids when they cashed in these 'credit hours'.

I confess, when I first launched into this way of doing things, my kids had a touch of 'cold turkey' from their lack of screen hours. It really was as if they had lost the ability to entertain themselves. I was shocked that I had not even previously realised how their time had been filled with so much nothingness. I'll be honest; it's my biggest parenting regret so far. Still, over time we built new routines and now 'screen time' is but a tiny player in the whole week. The option is to ditch the 'screen' altogether; this is becoming a more popular option than people would expect. What a daring opportunity to let your kids' imagination run free!

From one parent to another...

Sure, life without TV was difficult when they were all little. With five small children running around, at the time, it was tempting to turn on the TV just for a break. But the short term break would have created

a TV appetite in the children that we didn't want to feed. We reasoned that once they realized that the TV does most of the imagining and thinking for them their brains and bodies become lazy.

We have provided them with more meaningful alternatives than the one-eyed monster. Since the time they were little we have read books out loud as a family, played games, and filled their minds and time with more engaging activities. As a result, they are now young entrepreneurs with a host of hobbies that will provide enjoyment and income for the rest of their lives.

The sad reality is that the shows may be innocent or 'educational' when they are little but as they grow up so do their tastes. Barney may satisfy Junior when he's five, but when he's fifteen he is going to want to watch something a little more attractive than a purple dinosaur. The problem is that his habits have been established and his appetite to be entertained has been satisfied for so many years he doesn't know what to do with himself.

It doesn't have to be this way. Take the time now to teach your young children how to control their appetites and allow them to feast on that which is good. A family snuggled together reading a book will keep even the youngest children engaged even without pictures if they are given the time to imagine. (I used to keep a stack of paper nearby while I was reading so they could colour and draw as they listened.) This is very labour intensive for the parents initially but once they have their appetite whetted for that which is truly good they will be less likely to desire the rancid food Hollywood dishes out.

Now that my children have become young adults their time is so filled up with so many other things of greater interest and the TV is not even of interest to them. They don't rush to see the latest episode of some show. I don't have to tell them 'NO you can't watch that' or 'no more TV today you've got to do your homework'. The goals and desires that they have set for themselves have made TV a distraction not an attraction. The idea of wasting hours in front of the TV is ludicrous to them.

Karen Braun, www.spunkyhomeschool.blogspot.com

Cool ideas factory

The first step in freeing up a kid's imagination is having a stimulating home environment. For me, this is more than simply finding something to keep the kids quiet for half an hour. 'What's the big deal?' some may ask. Well, we all make an effort to give them good nutrition, clean clothes. We decorate their bedrooms, ferry them around to their friends. Sparking and challenging their imagination? Well, they write stories at school, don't they? That's like saying good nutrition is only for lunchtime. I firmly believe that having an inspiring, vibrant family lifestyle will turbo-boost them academically. It will also encourage other diamond-encrusted characteristics such as being a self-starter, a problem solver, a communicator, an entrepreneur. A crucial part of this is to give them 'white space' time, where there is no entertainment on tap. Given enough of this space, and a generous dollop of inspiration, kids will eventually put the time to constructive use. It's a skill that can be learned at any time of life. Here are a few ideas...

- Have an 'inspiration wall'. Pick any wall in the house for anyone to stick things that inspire them (or in kidspeak 'cool pictures and stuff'). I casually mentioned we were going to do this with my kids. Then, without announcement, I stuck on some amazing surfing pictures. A week or so later, I took them off and stuck on an intricate piece of 3D space art. In case you're wondering, my kids don't clap their hands in glee at the prospect of an 'inspiration board'. They're more likely to give it a glance as they shuffle skateboard-wards. Yet as I make frequent changes to it (and it happens to be the wall opposite the table where they shovel in their breakfast cereal every morning), it has really caught their attention and initiated some interesting conversation. The great thing about this kind of wall is that it will be completely unique to each family. For my family, keeping it low key and 'mum's thing' has kept credibility.
- Leave a stash of boxes, string, springs etc. on the table occasionally.
- Get an unusual pet.
- Go for an adventure trek for the day. Pack up map, provisions and just go!
- Give them their own spot in the garden.
- Buy some oil paints and a canvas and create a 'family' piece of art for the wall.
- Get a book about science experiments using home ingredients.
- Announce Friday is cook day and each child, in turn, cooks the main meal on a Friday.

Depending on age you can give more or less supervision on buying ingredients/cooking/serving/washing up.

- Join the local nature club.
- Set up a homemade weather station in the garden (lots of online resources for this).
- I met one family who had a yearly 'dad and kid' weekend away. Each year it was a child's turn to have a weekend away with dad (there were four kids in the family).
- 'Scrapbooking' is a hobby that is growing in popularity worldwide. It's about creating an original family book with photos and mementoes.
- Create a 'memory jar' using coloured sand or salt. Each layer in a different colour reminds you of special occasions.
- Start a family diary together and jot down everyday or funny happenings.
- Go out for a late-night walk.
- Create a special family celebration day, e.g. the budgie's birthday, gaining a swimming badge.

For these ideas and more, check out www.careforthe family.org – a highly recommended family resource.

Family memories – gold dust of our kids' world

In the world of property development, 'home staging' is a buzz phrase. The idea is to make the property as pleasant as possible – plenty of magnolia paint and scented soap blocks. Clothes over the radiators, body board stashed behind the sofa, toys on the stairs would be a definite 'no-no'. 'House staging' makes houses look great, but it's not real life. Creating great family memories is not about 'staging' great moments or picture perfect outings. Sure, we can do a lot to initiate fun, reboot family life. However, the best memories are often the 'seize the moment' kind, sharing genuine fun in the hurly-burly of life. When we started our family I wondered how a child would fit into 'our' world. But in no time my little angel became a turbo charged individual who set to work creating his own universe and calling us to dive in with him. While disconcerting at times, it is exhilarating to watch your growing offspring launching into exploits you never would have enjoyed. Our kids have their own destiny, talents, likes and dislikes. Family 'time outs' should not have an agenda of pushing our kids in a particular direction. Kids can smell an agenda a mile away. Genuine wholehearted attention with no strings builds memories that are the gold dust of our kids' world.

The reality is this stuff doesn't take up much time at all; what it asks of us is to stretch our efforts to live a bit differently. Hands-on activity living is a really satisfying way to 'have house'. Some families naturally live this way; there's always a project on the go and lively debate over the dinner table. I have to really work on this stuff as I easily get distracted by the juggling call if I'm not careful. Nevertheless, work on it I will. My kids' imagination is far too precious.

From one parent to another...

When I was a child, the Children's museum was my absolute favourite place. I remember walking into the building and being in awe of the Allosaurus skeleton towering in the left window. Hanging from the ceiling was a huge biplane looking as if it were going to land right there in the building. To the right, there was an open, hands-on aquarium with starfish and other sea creatures. Over by the restrooms, there was another fish tank with a concave area where I could stick my head in and feel like I was inside the tank right along with the fish.

In that museum, I was transferred into a new world. There was the dark room with a dock leading to a ship complete with a navigation wheel waiting to be turned and a captain's quarters down below to explore. There were, what seemed like thousands, of stuffed wildlife on the walls above, ready to pounce on me if I lingered too long. There was the 'health room' where I crawled into a mouth many times and crawled out of the ear. I spent hours exploring the log cabin display, the half hewn Indian canoe.

I begged to go as often as I could and it always took some coaxing by my parents to get me out. This was the stuff of my childhood memories.

Unfortunately, somewhere around that time, the place caught on fire and the inside was gutted. It was never the same since. I went back one time after they reopened it and it was a major disappointment. Oh sure, the Allosaurus was still there, but gone were the imaginative displays and what replaced them was homogenized and pasteurized 'education'. The displays were reflections of a coming trend of 'scientific' hands-on learning. As educational as they may be, they lacked the imagination that creates a true learning experience for children. I doubt that any child attending these museums would have such a lasting and warm memory as this museum did for me.

Do yourself and your children a favour. Think about what kind of memories you want your children to have of their learning experiences and create that environment for them. They will cherish those memories as I do mine.

Wyndee Clara, www.homeschoolblogger.com/CMMomma

Turkey corkscrews

Jamie Oliver, a popular young British TV chef, is horrified about limp, fatty 'turkey corkscrews' on offer on school dinner menus. He reckons that many children eat junk because they don't have the opportunity to try tantalising, fresh food.

I had noticed that the quality of the books my eldest was choosing from the library were the type that are at home being a free gift on a breakfast cereal. 'Turkey corkscrew literature'. It began to bother me. We were raising our children on a junk literature diet of *Captain Underpants* and *Bratz*? What were they missing out on?

So, I set off to the library. As my boys gorged themselves on the video rental section and my toddler threw herself incessantly on the beanbags, I sat next to the potted plants and talked to Maggie, the librarian. She agreed that many modern kids' books are often shallow and recommended a selection of 'sheer genius' classics. Buoyed up, I rescued my red-faced toddler from the beanbags. Slapping my library card on the counter, I had a fleeting quiver of excitement, usually only reserved for the Monsoon sale. Could this humble collection of books represent something quite new for our family? Was it possible to escape, if only for ten minutes, from the rampant kid culture? Would their vivid imagination, long since buried, be re-ignited?

I pounced the next day in a ten-minute window between dinner and Cub Scouts. OK, I could have picked a more serene moment, but these are hard to come by in our house. I hid the TV remote, put a load of cushions on the floor and launched into *Swallows and Amazons*. Once the children had recovered from the hilarity that one of the characters is called Titty, we read and time seemed to disappear. I started to forge a new routine of family reading time each day. It took a huge amount of effort at first, but eventually 'the reading slot' became normal for all of us. We lost ourselves in the *Narnia Chronicles*, *The Railway Children* and *Little House on the Prairie*. We were hooked. By now, we were home-educating our turbocharged boys, and we soon realised what a brilliant history lesson classic literature provides. The historical detail was integral to the characters' lives; history in context 'for real'. The kids' concentration was soaring. I still read aloud to them every day; it's become a precious part of the day that none of us, especially the boys, would give up.

Kids who just don't want to do any inspiring/challenging/educational stuff

There's nothing worse than reading a chapter like this when you know that your own child would rather have a toenail removed than listen to you read *Swallows and Amazons*. They've had enough of 'school stuff' and they are not interested in any activities you have concocted. In fact they'd rather you took up flower arranging (anything!) other than plan stuff that might impede on 'their' time. OK, kids don't need to be cornered and pounced on. Respect goes a long way when you have a resistant kid. However (and this is a HUGE however), I would suggest that unless the kid in question is 18, it's possibly the biggest parenting mistake we could make to allow them to opt out of family life to 'do life' with their friends. If this is the case, the kid in effect is being raised by his peers. Their lifestyle choices will directly impact him. His choices in everything – from sex to career choice – will be influenced primarily by passing kids. Sure, he has his independence – but at what cost?

For this kid, and indeed most I've come across, the 'chilled approach' to imagination boosting is the way forward. For my bunch, leaving stuff out that might catch their eye works really well. Some kids might enjoy an adult exploring new stuff alongside them; others like having friends round for a papier-mâché party. The main point here is – do new and challenging stuff WITH your kids. Whether it's keeping stick insects, doing mosaic, building a huge Lego construction – JUST DO IT! Even the most lethargic, resistant kid will become intrigued.

Getting knee-deep and dirty (from the biggest hygiene freak on the planet)

I once went to visit a friend and while we sipped coffee her boy was in the garden doing mud sculpture. I'm not talking 'sculpture' along the lines of magnificent ice sculptures you see at the winter Olympics. These sculptures (as far as I could see) were piles of mud sitting in a dirty pool of water with a few stones lobbed on top. Of course when the inevitable 'Mom! Jane! Come and see what I've sculpted!' shout came I dutifully trotted out and 'oohhed' and 'ahhhed' with his mom (although I think she actually meant it). I confess my hygiene freak tendencies were out in full force and it was as much as I could do to not stop him putting his fingers near his mouth. Had they not heard of rotavirus? Cat pooh? Why couldn't he just do a nice playdough sculpture on a nice wipe-down table? The boy in question finally came in for lunch, and after a quick hand wash was at the table looking very grubby. Just like I just CAN'T watch my husband take his contact lenses out, I just couldn't watch this child eat.

I've thrown in this story for you (yes, I know I'm uptight) just to remind you that I am so not a 'let it all hang out' earth mother just in case you might think this is the case as I discuss the benefits of getting knee-deep and dirty. There is a HUGE benefit to kids just being out in nature exploring. While every person would agree kids need time in the great outdoors (the local play park doesn't count), it can easy become one of those 'to do' things that hum away on the back burner but never actually touch base with real life on a regular basis.

Getting out in nature has now become to me like going to a spa, the theatre or other complete indulgences. Despite my hygiene freak tendencies, I just love it. Sure, I take copious supplies of wet wipes, plasters and Kleenex. I doubt if I'll ever make the grade of 'earth mother', but the enjoyment can't be beat. Sure, it gets you fit and all that, but the outdoor life is fun – and that's much more of a pull for me. Another fun thing that I tried is keeping a 'nature notebook' with the kids. Along the same lines as the 'inspiration wall' this is a scrapbook-style compilation of drawings, photos, art ,descriptions of things discovered on our nature treks. Again with this one, I did the leg work – I got a big scrapbook, my youngest 'decorated' it with dried grasses, and I labelled it 'OUR FAMILY NATURE NOTEBOOK' and put it in my bag for one of our walks. As I sat sketching a nest for the book, the kids soon wanted a piece of the action and begged for a piece of paper and a pencil, each of which 'luckily' I had stashed in my bag (hey, maybe I will make it as an 'earth mother' one day!). A year or so later, we have a wonderfully unique record of our discoveries. I guess one day when my kids are grown, I'll love looking at this, like hand-drawn pictures – and so will they!

An unexpected bonus of a nature notebook is something happens that teachers will spend hours trying to achieve. Different subjects correlate – scientific observation, drawing, writing, poetry and natural history all come together. It's amazing! This isn't just for forest walks – sparrows, ants, park trees, weather, astronomy are fascinating if we just pause for a moment to look!

One chickpea short of a casserole?

My eldest started school with a wide-eyed curiosity for all things new and interesting. However, as the years ticked by, we noticed his curiosity and zest for life wane a little. Rather than the social feast the playground was meant to be, it appeared it was peer pressure all the way.

His imaginative play was gradually being replaced my mindless silliness. For sure, you could argue that this change in his character was just him growing up and getting a taste of the 'real world'. Something about this logic didn't sit quite right, but I couldn't quite put my finger on it. Life was a hectic business of picking up, dropping off, packing lunchboxes and snatching family time together before bed. It wasn't until I relaxed over a latte one evening that all my concerns about delegating Joseph's education away came tumbling out of my heart like Labrador puppies. By then, his peers were the major influences in his world. Was this the best way to raise a child? Being curious was no longer 'cool', in his opinion. Was the 'de-programming' I found myself doing as he got home from school to reset a decent attitude really the best way forward? We've all heard the proverb, Train a child in the way he should go' (Proverbs 22:6). I realised that the state and his peers were raising him the majority of his waking hours; that was the 9am to 4pm reality.

As the questions tumbled out, I even surprised myself. School, I had always believed, was the only reasonable path for raising a balanced kid, able to hold his own in the world. Raising a child able to reach his academic potential was a big deal to me. Just as it was a big deal that my child could hold his own in the rough and tumble of life with other kids. However, the school system seemed to deliver more disadvantages than advantages. Rather than developing robust social skills, it seemed to be a breeding grounds for negative social skills such as disrespect for authority. Remember here, I'm no earth mother, just your average kind of girl. So, where to go with these rampant concerns? Well, I did what any hardcore juggler would do: put my concerns on the back burner and got on with life.

That was a few years ago. After months of soul searching we ended up homeschooling our motley tribe. Before you skip this bit expecting me to launch off into rampant organic ramblings, I'm not going to. When I say that we home educate, most people assume that we are obsessed parents, or live in a tepee. Either way, the assumption is that we must be one chickpea short of a casserole! For what it's worth, I'm still the same life-loving girl who believes a good education is absolutely crucial. We, like millions of families worldwide, have opted for an education path that is actually research-proven to deliver academic and social advantage. My kids are doing pretty well; we do lots of hands-on projects, trips and learning in context. We have a crazily busy social calendar and with Boy Scouts, tennis, badminton, karate and kids' clubs, it makes for a full life. We often 'do school' with other families, which is great fun. I now share my kitchen with a bunch of science-crazed explorers, my garden with a bunch of naturalists, and my sitting room with a ton of Lego (not forgetting Virgil the snail).

When all is said and done...

Having a home life that is merely a pit stop for family members is a great tragedy. Sure, we all have different interests, responsibilities and schedules. Yet, if quality time has somehow slipped off the priority list it's time to haul it back in there. Quality family time roots children and gives them memories that will strengthen them throughout life. Family time is crucial to our kids' academic and social development. I encourage you to keep a lid on the influence of media in your home; instead, turn your home into a cool ideas factory! Try reading to your kids, there's nothing like it. Inspiring creativity in family life will result in entrepreneurs, scientists and future leaders.

One unexpected bonus of regular muddy treks into the great outdoors and trips to vast museums is that something changed in my heart. I guess, the bigger picture of the world, its seasons and delights, made me a bit less preoccupied with the ins and outs of my own life. While on one hand, I think we have stretched our intellect (certainly our bodies) in the discovery of new things, we are also realising how the world doesn't actually revolve around us.

'Do you wish to become great?' asks St Augustine. 'Then begin by little. Do you desire to construct vast lofty fabric? Think first about the foundations of humility. The higher the structure is to be, the deeper must be its foundation.'

If you want great things for your kids – great choices, great relationships, great home life, great career – the foundation to build is the appreciation of the magnificence of the world we have been given. Then, any greatness that may arise will not be based on self-promotion, but on the appreciation that we are precious and indeed blessed. We can't change the tides, dictate the weather, cancel out the sun, and explain the intricacies of how birds know where to migrate. Humility is the beginning of true greatness.

This is heavy stuff from a girl sitting in the corner of

Starbucks noisily sucking a Frappucino through a straw. But hey, we get one shot at life, so why not reach for the stars? Beginning with our own backyard.

6

For your eyes only

The biggest tragedy for any lifelong multi-tasker is that she gets so swamped by pressing needs that her own sense of 'self' gets lost. She becomes like a steel reinforced ship, riding wave after wave, buffeted this way and that. She needs to gingerly climb out of the boat, and re-inhabit her body. This chapter is about taking ownership of the skin that we're in. Looking after your soft tender self is worth as much focus and effort as any other aspect of being a great parent. Indeed, without cherishing yourself, you can't truly cherish your family.

Sweet, sweet silence

The twin beds were inches apart and appeared to be welded to the chalet wardrobes. Ten years ago I would've been attacking the wardrobes with a power saw so I could sleep in my husband's arms. Yet in France last summer, the prospect of spending seven days in a hard, thin, plastic-covered BED OF MY OWN filled me with secret delight. A whole week without sleep-sodden mumblings of work schedules. Seven whole nights without somebody else's head on my pillow. *Magnifique!*

When we had tiny babies ANY sleep was a bonus and sleep became something that occasionally filled the gaps between wails. Now (with any luck) little night-time visitors are less frequent, and I like it. Maybe that's why delicious sleep is my sanctuary – less chance of a juggling moment finding me out! A moment of uninterrupted stillness just can't be beat (as long as it doesn't last too long!).

Busyness whispers to us that we are needed. It's easy to moan about how many emails we have to write, yet none of us like a silent inbox. While we may complain there are too many demands on us, when none are made it's easy to feel unimportant. We all need to pause and consider: 'Is there a quiet breeze underneath the thrashing whirlwind of my life? Is there a point where my life is rooted and from which I can live in security and confidence?'

'Rushaholic' world

There's 'time out' and there's 'time out'. 'Grade A time out' helps us touch base with the stuff of life that really matters; we recharge and take time just to be with God. It's the place where that quiet breeze tickles our ears and we drink deep and our souls are blessed. 'Grade B time out' usually begins as 'Grade A' but slips into 'Grade B' as we find ourselves being distracted, or using the time to have a stealthy de-junk of the kids' bedrooms. The 'rushaholic' world lures us away. Now, friend, I've been honest with you up to now on the reality of my life versus the perfect image of a parenting author. I'd love to smugly describe how my life is sparkling with 'Grade A' fairy dust. Alas, often the closest I get to being this fairy is prancing around the lounge wearing a pink feather boa to keep my daughter quiet so I can answer the phone to an editor without him thinking *Sesame Street* is my background music of choice. You see, currently, my life goes as follows:

- 6.45 – Wake up. Drag self out of bed. Assess bad hair day stakes.
- 7.00 – Open all curtains, get kids to do chores, make breakfast. It's a tough choice between healthy muesli option and glow-in-the-dark kids' cereal. Fix daughter's hair (old lady next door considers calling police), empty dishwasher and get a free steam facial (multi-tasking bonus there).
- 8.00 – All have breakfast. Do school.
- 13:00 – Kids have half-hour quiet time in rooms. I get half an hour break. Perfect 'Grade A time out' opportunity but the chances are I'll run round like a lunatic throwing washing into the machine and doing general high-octane juggling.
- 14:00 – Take kids to meet their friends and head off to woods/museum/theatre/assault course/pond dipping.
- 16:00 – Get home, throw dinner in oven. With any luck I'll remember to turn oven on.
- 18.30 – Husband home. All eat dinner together. Plenty of action varying from fun to stressful.
- 19.00 – Marathon of kids in bed, stories, checking for Daleks under the bed.

- **20.00 – Unearth my laptop from piles of kid junk. Panic when find a kid has been downloading Sonic the Hedgehog games. Honestly, if you are reading this without huge runs of Sonic downloaded all over it, either a miracle has taken place or my editor had his finger on the delete key for a very long time.**
- **Write 1,000 words a night on this book. Check emails. Quick peak on eBay for some decadent purchase I will certainly regret.**
- **22.00 – Chill out with husband.**
- **23.00 – Crash into bed.**

Where do I squeeze some decent 'Grade A time out' into all of that? I don't seem to be any busier than my friends who are all dressed and ready by 7am and fall into bed around midnight with the washing machine still churning, the tumble drier thumping and dishwasher whirring. According to Carl Honore, author of *In Praise of Slow* (Orion), we inhabit a 'rushaholic world' in which 'the cult of speed can only get worse. When everyone takes the fast option, the advantage of going fast vanishes, forcing us to go faster still.' Hectic schedules cause us to lose touch with friends and miss opportunities. The average lunch hour is 27 minutes, and we have less and less time to cook. We are urged to slow down, to set priorities and limits.

Escaping 'rushaholism'

Italy, the land of outdoor living, has created the concept of the 'slow city' movement. Now 64 places worldwide have been given the 'slow city' status, with strict requirements of a population less that 50,000; standard of air quality; level of noise pollution; and availability of locally sourced food. I'm lucky enough to live in a village with a butcher, greengrocer all sourced locally. However, the closest I get to these shops is when I whiz past on my way to Asda Wal-Mart, or when I pop in for special occasion food. So, not one to dish out advice I can't take, I'm going to do the 'slow living thing' for the next month and let you know how I get on.

One month later...

Entry 1

First morning I stayed in bed while husband made me a cup of tea (be impressed). I sipped the hot brew listening to the birds outside and woke up slowly – I could get used to this. Husband, buoyed by his 'I made her a morning cup of tea' status, throws on his clothes and hops it to work. I float downstairs at the time I'm usually ready to start the day and find kids cross-eyed with two hours straight of *Spongebob Squarepants*, solidified breakfast cereal in bowls, no curtains open. It's lunchtime before I'm sorted. Not a happy bunny. My relaxation credits just weren't worth the fallout. Next time I'll request kids' breakfast and dressing supervision as a more valuable option.

Entry 2

Bought all meat from local butcher, fruit and vegetables from farm shop. Felt very smug, and the food was indeed so much better than pre-packed supermarket equivalent. Found following a recipe very relaxing and the food was so great the extra effort was so worth it. Ignored kids' pleas for fish finger reinstatement.

Got a board game out of the loft for us all to play this evening. Expected boys to snort in disgust as they thundered skateboard-wards, was pleasantly surprised as they dived in. Weekend: instead of charging off to the swimming pool for a chlorine fix and a faceful of other people's kids, we headed off to a safari park. All was going wonderfully until the baboons started getting passionate on the bonnet, and the rubber ring around the aerial got swiped by a monkey who looked suspiciously like a neighbour's kid.

Entry 3

I might have cracked it. Decided not to go to parks with primary-coloured equipment for a while. They're always busy, noisy, and have ice cream vans poised at all the exits. Where's the break in that? So went to parkland, rivers, anywhere where there was space. I was enjoying it so much that I barely noticed the kids were having such a great time dashing through the trees. Getting away from it all is definitely a 'slow down' option that works for me.

Entry 4

Next evening, instead of working, I take up a friend's offer of coffee at Starbucks (like I was going to refuse that!). I should be enjoying the froth and conversation but I'm twitching and surreptitiously checking my watch. I should be working. I have words to write. I down my coffee in one.

Entry 5

Well, there's something to be said about shopping from a butcher and farm shop. I've now got quite chummy with the bearded lady at the farm shop. I don't even hold my breath when she muscles up close to show me how to dig deep into the carrot sack to get the best 'corkers'. OK, so my stomach still turns that I have no choice but to choose eggs with feathers stuck on (stuck on with WHAT exactly?) but I'm a darn sight closer to nature than my previous token gestures.

OK, month over... this slow-living business is hard work! I guess that's part of the point; 'fast living' is about expending the least effort possible because the next task is pending. While slow living was 'harder' work it was satisfying in a long-walk-in-mountains kind of a way. I confess I had moments of teeth-grinding frustration at other people's slow living. Sure, it's quaint that our butcher chats about village life with customers as he gift-wraps their fillets, but I found it mind-bendingly frustrating to wait meekly as he kept rewrapping the fillets to get them symmetrical.

Fast meets slow

Most of us with busy lives and even busier kids would consider the 'slow living' option as an unrealistic option long term. Maybe the answer is to weave in some slow living into a busy life. For example, sitting in the garden with a book for half an hour before picking the kids up. In little bite-sized chunks these 'go slow moments' make a real difference. A major issue for many burnt-out parents who have lost the knack of going slow is that they have lost the sense of their own interests and talents. Life just sucked it all away. Well, the good news is that incorporating 'slow living' moments into daily life has an amazing effect of re-igniting talent that was previously lost. Would you like to try your hand at art? Fashion? Writing? Sculpting? Take little windows of slow living and who knows what may be around the corner? A friend of mine took the time to go swimming, by herself, twice a week. By taking this step, she soon found that she had the confidence to try hat designing again, a talent of her youth. It's a matter of making space for the things that matter.

What tickles your fancy?

Discipline is one of those words that's as tricky to spell as it is to pull off. It's something I'm going to have to dish out right now as my kids are currently launching snails over the garden fence. Yes, friend, that's what my dear darlings are doing right now as I snatch time to write this. They think I can't see, but whispering 'Throw it higher and it might land on the shed' is just too much of a giveaway…. I'll be back in a minute. There, job done; the snail population is breathing a sigh of relief. Where was I? Discipline. HA!

Well, not kid discipline, for a change, but the grown-up stuff, the self-discipline stuff that means we keep our word to ourselves. You see, I think many of us use the fact that we juggle as one almighty excuse not to take ownership of our lives and make the changes necessary to make our lives better. Sometimes we actually choose the franticness of life, because it gives us an opt-out clause for facing our realities. The key to self-discipline is to NOT automatically satisfy any desire that tickles our fancy. Juggling frenzy can be such that people don't distinguish what they'd quite like to do and what's good to do. So they do it all, and sort out the consequences afterwards. We CAN choose to have, and choose when not to have. The benefits of living a measured life are not boring, they are liberating. When we satisfy any want we have just because we want it, life actually ends up pretty meaningless. It's also the quickest way to get screwed up financially, emotionally and physically. After all, how can we expect our kids to make good choices in life, when we ourselves abandon ourselves to whatever catches our eye? It takes conscious effort and a dollop of restraint to incorporate slow living into a fast-paced life. Is this self-discipline thing worth it? What do you reckon!

The guilt mojo

After the snail chucking episode my kids wandered inside and hung around me. I was torn between frustration that my peaceful zone was lost, and being kind of chuffed that my mommy magnet proved strong even when I had just spoiled their fun. What followed was the routine they have down to a fine art. 'Mom, do you want to play a game? Mom, can we go to the shop and get a comic? Mom, can we have a cake, we're HUNGRY!' The aim of this relentless barrage of questions is that they reckon I'll say 'yes' to one of the questions just for some peace. After many years of building my mommy muscles I now have no qualms about saying 'NO' to 99 percent of demands. This, however, doesn't stop a nugget of guilt stubbing my conscience regularly.

Guilt is the nugget that whispers 'How could you consider reading a book in the garden when there's so much laundry to do?'

The only real type of guilt that we should listen to is that still small voice that niggles away when we have done something genuinely wrong. I have developed a bit of a radar for my own guilt mojo. If guilt pops into my head I'll pause, assess whether I'm just being too hard on myself, or whether I actually need to address something. seventy percent of the time, guilt is because I don't give myself a break, so I send it packing.

On-the-spot living

For many parents, reacting to the things that crop up in the day means very little space is left for the things that really matter. This way of living is called 'fire fighting' and prioritising happens on the spot as things happen. Sure, we all have days like this, but it's a poor way to live long term. 'Fire fighting' happens when life is approached reactively, rather than proactively. To be proactive means to 'exercise your freedom of choice with appropriate assertiveness and direct your life according to actual needs, desires and hopes without being unduly concerned or swayed by other people's opinions and expectations'. To be reactive means to 'go through life with little sense of control, just reacting to things as they come along.' Reactive living leaves little room for 'time out'. Sometimes we just need to make a moment of time out a real priority to see the balls more clearly.

From one parent to another...

Some people enjoy taking a walk, others going for a ride. I'm not really a mall gal, walking is exercise, and bookstores are dangerous places for our budget. I love going for rides, but that's more of a weekend kind of thing that I love sharing with my husband. For me, it's a trip to the coffee shop.

For a few dollars I 'rent' a table in air conditioned/heated comfort and enjoy something hot or cold to drink depending on the season/ weather. It's where I hang out while my son is at choir practice. Oh, sure I could run all kinds of errands during that time, but ever since my boys were in Karate, I've taken their extra curricular lessons time as a time to read, catch my breath, stare out of a big picture window and dream, or some other form of relaxation. I cherish and am thankful for this time. And I think it's a necessary time. This past year especially, with our house moving/ renovation project, our lives are very hectic. I spend most of my time with my husband and/or kids, and as much as I absolutely love being with them most of every day, it is nice to have some 'down' time. Time spent without answering questions, thinking through problems, or planning ahead. Time spent reading, daydreaming, or writing my thoughts down.

It makes me think of the importance of defending our children's window to be children – time to play, explore nature, and just daydream. It also makes me understand grandparents just a bit better. They are at the stage of life where they realise what is really important in life: time to pause and reflect, time to stare out a window, time to just enjoy the gift of life.

I'm trying to learn and embrace that lesson now (before becoming a grandparent!), with my family and make sure that each one from my husband to my youngest take time to breathe deeply, relax wearied minds and bodies, and enjoy the bountiful gifts for rich and poor, young and old alike: sunshine; flowers; soft breezes; pools and streams of water; blue skies and thunderstorms. And sometimes a trip to the coffee shop.

Sheryl Rogener,
www.homeschoolblogger.com/takingthechallenge

Big knickers

I have been likened to Bridget Jones so many times that I'm going to surrender and talk about big knickers. Real big belly huggers, like those maternity ones made out of white teabag material. Big knickers, the saggier the better. A greying shade of white would be good, and also an equally greying bra, straps slightly fraying. These are the secret reality of life when life gets so frantic, the woman hasn't snatched time or cash to look after herself. Now don't give me baloney about not having enough money. We're not talking designer thongs in raw silk here, just knickers that are worthy of you. Beautiful, magnificent you.

When all is said and done...

I'm a sucker for quick fixes. Yet we all know there is no quick fix for trading a crazy juggling life for a satisfyingly full, yet calm one. It takes effort, decision and change. When our lives are like saucepans full of boiling water about to bubble over at any minute, ANYTHING extra to think about seems like it will send our saucepans bubbling over everywhere! Yet there is one chink of light at the end of the tunnel. This chink is especially for the days when all this downshifting seems like just too much effort. This one simple step somehow seems to make the rest of the pieces of life settle into the right place. Here it is... Cherish yourself. Allot time for yourself, give yourself priorities, limits. Why? Because you are precious and wonderfully made. Realise this, and somehow the stuff of family life seems to start heading in the right direction. I guess the psychology boffins would say that boosting your self-esteem will automatically give a greater sense of control in other areas of life. I like to think of it as like lying on my back in a field watching birds swoop around. The front one heads in a direction and the others follow gracefully, as if they are moving as one. Get the 'I am precious and wonderfully made' part as a priority and life just flows better. Sure, it's always going to be bursting at the seams. But maybe, just a sharpening of focus and choosing to hold dear the stuff that really matters, is all it will take to make the ride more of a thrill than a stress.

From one parent to another...
A moment to myself... well, almost

Wake to kids' music and screams coming from the living room. Lift your head (sorta) off the pillow and bellow for everyone to be quiet. Stumble to the bathroom then check on the noise and find everyone dancing and singing to a CD. Grunt at them when they tell you good morning.

Tell everyone to get their books and get ready for school while you shower. Somehow, in their Charlie Brown world, they translate that to BEGIN their school work.

Get in shower and turn the water on hot to try and clear your head. Hear a voice nearby. Peek out of the curtain to find 7 year old sitting on your toilet – using it – and reading his science book to you. Learn about the water cycle while you shower. Take an extra long shower, because 7 year old is concentrating on reading instead of doing his business. Eventually realize you have time to shave your legs because he is still reading. Start shaving.

While leaned over shaving, have 6 year old come into the bathroom (at which point 7 year old screams like a girl although he isn't and throws a towel over his lap). 6 year old has arrived to discuss blend sounds so she can do her phonics book. Try to distinguish between the pr and tr blend sounds being made by a child with a speech problem – over the sound of water running and 7 year old reading aloud. Peek out, trying to read the page without your bifocals on, as water drips off your hair onto the page. See that she can do the next page without your help. Tell her to do the next page and you will go back and help her with the one she skipped in a few minutes. Watch – though not in surprise – as she turns around and runs to flop herself on your bed to wait for you.

Next, have 5 year old come in with his time and money book. 7 year old still on toilet, 6 year old on bed and 5 year old has decided it is time to learn 'more than the hour and half hour' page. Guess it is a new year's resolution or something. While speaking very loudly to be heard over the water cycle and the 6 year old doing phonics on the bed, you try to explain that each number is worth five minutes. Not working. Water is starting to grow cold.

Here is where the older child helping the younger child comes into play that we have all heard so much about. 7 year old – still on the toilet – removes wall clock and putting aside his science book onto the sink, begins to explain time to the 5 year old, moving the clock hands to demonstrate 5 minute increments. After a few minutes – or 50 depending on which clock you look at, the water is tepid and along comes another 5 year old to join your merry group.

He brings the cool new Logico learning system with him. The card he has in his hand consists of an animal mixed up – the head of one animal and the body of another. His job – should he choose to do it in the bathroom – is to find the two animals that comprise this animal and mark them accordingly. Everyone rushes to help – the 7 year old puts the clock back on the wall – somewhat crookedly because it is over his head and backwards, but up, nonetheless. By now, you have shaved everything but your head, thoroughly conditioned your hair, and scrubbed the tub walls clean. The water is cold and so are you. You are now ready to abandon this tiny one room schoolhouse for another room. You tell everyone to leave. The 7 year old is still not done, so he hands you a towel in the shower and you wrap your body in the towel and get out.

You send everyone out of your bedroom back to the kitchen to wait for you. You put lotion on your feet – almost – before the 6 year old is back. She wants to rub the lotion in for you. Not wanting to start an argument – you agree. You're half dressed before the 5 year olds are back. One to show you his correct Logico page and the other to show you what page he is going to do in his math book... but first he wants to read to you. So he crawls up on the bed and begins to read – competing with the 7 year old who is now reading about plants and their need for water – of which you now have only cold. You send the 6 year old off – again – who quickly returns with a story book which she pretends to read to you – louder than the 5 year old and the 7 year old. You put on deodorant – which is always a show stopper, because everyone wants deodorant on. After deodorizing and powdering everyone, applying face cream to yourself and the 6 year old, you finally finish dressing. Tell the 7 year old to get done. NOW.

Then you decide to dry your hair – not because it is part of your morning routine – but only to drown out the readers and have a moment of quiet... Well, almost!

Perri Huddleston, www.homeschoolblogger.com/perri

7

Parenting hot potatoes

Most of us are just about juggling all the balls of life and have little time to consider any right or wrong approaches to parenting. After all, why make a roller coaster journey even more complicated? Well, here's a reason: If there is a wealth of information out there that would improve family life, I want to know about it. If new information challenges my current way of doing things, I still want to know about it! So this chapter is going to explore some of the tricky parenting issues that often get ignored, the parenting 'hot potatoes'. Feeling brave? Dive in!

Fast-moving world

I like my tumble drier. Not only is it great for soggy towels on a rainy day, it also whips the laundry round at such a frenzy that if you catch it at the right moment you just don't have to iron it. I guess I'm a life-loving vixen who loves her gadgets that free me up for more exciting stuff. Abundant technology is the stamp of the developed world, resulting in more opportunities and careers than ever before. I spoke to someone recently, however, who had jacked in his high-flying commuter lifestyle to go help build a hospital in an Indonesian rainforest. He shared stories of eating wild boars, carving out canoes and the skill of the barefoot huntsmen. He observed kids being raised by a combination of parents, siblings, relatives and community members. Mothers would carry toddlers in slings; older boys accompanied the men throughout the day. When the child became an adult he got married young, then started a whole new team. Life was simply about putting food on the table and the needs of the community. This has been the pattern of life the world over until quite recently.

The 1960s heralded momentous breakthroughs in the West, not least the invention of beehive hairstyles and the beginnings of the huge technology boom. Then followed a huge increase in both parents working outside the home. In response to this, there has been a tremendous rise in childcare provision. Consequently, a parent can have their child cared for from six weeks after birth till school age 8am to 6pm every day. Then 15,000 hours of school till they're 16 years old, and activities clubs every night of the week. This an extreme example, but a notable shift in our generation is that most children spend more time away from family than ever before. Some kids only eat at home on weekends! Now I know I'm in a 'hot potato' zone, and there is much to be said for the modern opportunities the world offers our kids. Nevertheless, I do wonder about the lifelong impact of our generation's reliance on childcare. This leads us to our first 'hot potato'...

Hot potato: Outsourcing parenting

I'm a hard-working mum with a fistful of kids in a real world and I know full well how parents have to put food on the table. Nevertheless, I still think that kids are always better off being cared for by someone who actually loves them. Stimulating surroundings, while important, don't touch on the question of love. Children can be safe, stimulated and entertained, but their deeper, more subtle needs cannot be met except by someone with a fierce, long-term commitment to them. This is not something any establishment can provide. Consistent stability, the very foundation of a child's world, is impossible to achieve in a childcare institution. Even in exceptionally highly rated establishments, the child is cared for by many different carers during his formative years. It is my belief that full-time childcare is primarily about a convenient service for the parents, not about meeting the child's needs.

You don't often hear about concerns over outsourcing parenting, because no one wants to make a working parent feel guiltier. Nor, indeed, do I. Yet I think it's a bit patronising that the documented disadvantages of childcare are pushed under the carpet in case they offend. We parents care intensely about our children and deserve to be well informed about the whole picture and the impact on our kids of our choices. These issues are not only relevant to parents of under-fives. There is just as much opportunity for older kids to spend more time in school, clubs and activities than they do touching base with their family. Sure, there are social and sporting benefits to these events. I just think we need to be so wary of loss of time to connect with parents and siblings, and to develop their own hobbies out of the glare of peer pressure. Do you catch my drift? Is there not a danger that our kids are in the care of so many different adults throughout the week that they become masters of autopilot living – the very thing we are trying to escape?

From one parent to another...

A few months ago a mother came to me all excited. She began to tell me about an experience she had in her daughter's primary school.

It was around Christmas and her daughter came home from school telling her mom all the wonderful stories her teacher had been reading to her. Sadly, the daughter lamented however, none of the stories were about the real Christmas story. The daughter asked her mother if she could come to her class and read to her a story from their shelf about the real Christmas story. The mother thoughtfully replied that she would love to but that she would have to check with the teacher. The daughter seemed satisfied. The mother approached the teacher about the matter. The teacher told her that any extra reading material had to be cleared by the headteacher. The mother appealed to the headteacher who then consulted with a guideline for reading. After a short wait the mother was granted her request on the grounds that the birth was historical in nature. The mother was thankful.

Not wanting to burst her enthusiasm I told her how glad I was that she was able to read to the children. The mother's excitement puzzled me. Why would a mother seek the authority of someone else to read a book to her child and the classroom? The answer is obvious, of course. The mother was not the authority in the classroom. This is as it should be. The mother is not there every day and the teacher must keep control of the room and the headteacher must keep control of the school. The mother rightly sought their approval because that is the system that she submitted to when she allowed her daughter to attend.

The question is, why would a mother knowingly yield her authority to someone else to the point where a simple request for a story would require the approval of three others?

Are we knowingly giving the job of raising our children over to another?

We don't readily admit this of course. But the increased reliance on day care, before school, and after school programs demonstrates something else. There are companies that will send a day care provider (paid for by the company) to the house when a child is ill so that mum can still go to work. Many children will grow up having more memories of a childcare provision than they will of home.

Childcare is not the only arena that our generation is doing this. We don't want the inconvenience of monitoring our children's viewing habits so we expect others to rate the shows for us and then we will decide based on their standard. Never mind that their standard is not ours, they saved us the time necessary to do it ourselves. We feel good that we have done something and we are thankful.

We rely on internet filters to strain out the filth from our computers. Sure they miss some things that we wouldn't approve of, but we're willing to make the trade off for the convenience of not having to monitor ourselves. We can go on with our own business because someone else is 'parenting' the children and we are thankful. We are thankful when schools monitor children's health, teach them about sex and relationships, and offer before and after school care.

Are we outsourcing parenting?

Karen Braun, www.spunkyhomeschool.blogspot.com

Hot potato: 'Stranger danger'

According to a bird-watching friend of mine, eagles have quite a shocking habit. When a little eaglet reaches a certain age the mother eagle shoves it out of the nest. Remember here that eagles nest at the top of precipices so our little eaglet with stumpy wings is hurtling towards certain doom. Until, that is, another eagle from the flock swoops in at the last moment and takes the dazed chick back up to the nest. Then, the whole merry game is repeated. What amazes me the most is that the mother eagle trusts another member of the eagle community to swoop in and save the day. Believe it or not, the result of all this high-octane action is that the eaglet finally learns to fly. Where I'm heading with this is the huge value of good one-to-one role models for kids. A good role model is one who has the same standards and beliefs as the parent; one who is confident in his own identity; and is empathetic and encouraging to the child. For children wishing to spread their wings, an outing with such a person can do wonders for the child's confidence and self-esteem. It's well worth considering what any adult interacting with your child 'brings to the table' as far as positive qualities go. It's all very well sticking your child in a football club if he has a talent for it, but if the coach is an intolerant bully it will do more to cement bad attitudes in your kid. Surely, this is not outweighed by being able to shoot a few goals!

Sometimes a close relative or friend would very much like to take a child under their wing, but is wary of broaching this in our 'stranger danger' society. Sadly, this is a real sticking point in our world. What a tragedy if our kids miss out on fishing for a mackerel, chopping logs, learning how to skateboard, even clearing out a shed with someone with a genuine heart for your family. When a known adult takes one of my tribe on an activity or job, it feels really good. I don't usually subscribe to the 'if it feels good, do it' way of living, but something about genuine community spirit really warms my soul. In our crazy juggling frenzy of a world it's very easy to forget the value of community. We're not little islands bumping into each other now and again. Throughout history, kids have grown in stature through the wise counsel and learning of community members. A sense of involvement in community would not only give our kids a sense of root and identity, but also a sense of responsibility to younger members. All good stuff for raising them to live life to the full, rather than be life-tourists!

Now you could say all this community talk is only for rainforest families, and those already in close-knit communities. Indeed, many of us live in a chaotic world that is far from the idyllic picture of kids learning to bake around a neighbour's stove. Certainly, it's only right that we are alert in a 'stranger danger' society and raise our children to be responsible in this area. However, it is sad if an inflated fear of 'stranger danger' actually stops us involving our children in the local community. The elderly in particular have a wealth of wisdom and stories to share. Looking at the bigger picture, these life stories are heritage from one generation to the next; they shouldn't be ignored. While it is true that many of us live fast-paced lives, it is also true that we can all find someone kind-hearted enough to share a little wisdom from their world with our kids. I recently asked a dear elderly lady for tea to share her childhood war stories with my kids. Not only was she thrilled at the invitation, my kids got their first glimpse of the sacrifice many made for their country. I also know a guy who has an allotment, and I'm planning on asking if we can go help him out one day. Our communities are full of people quietly doing their own thing who would love to share a tidbit of their passion. Sometimes, it's just a matter of asking.

Hot potato: Under-fives

OK, so I can't avoid any longer the raising of issues of those cute little sanity-hijackers we call toddlers. We're talking the chubby-kneed variety that knee-skid around the house and post raisins into the DVD player at each pit stop. Don't be fooled that it's all innocent cherubs can manage at their age. At bedtime they whip out a checklist of exact requirements – a book that they know ALL the words to; soft toy of specified species; blanket with soggy corner on the top right; particular side of pillow facing uppermost; milk heated to regulation temperature in non-microwaveable beaker; and rigorous monster-under-the-bed check. Then they wake you up at 5am by launching Buzz Lightyear down the stairs 'to infinity and beyond!!' Well, these are the little infiltrators of family life who would very much like to call the shots on the 'raising of children' front. Yes, they are cute, and asleep, they leave us breathless and devoted. Their sweet little habits and made-up words are so mesmerising, that if they were available in tablet form they'd be illegal.

The answer to successful family life when a toddler is lurking in your midst? Raise them the way they should go – don't let them call the shots. Why are toddlers in the chapter on parenting hot potatoes? Because, despite the glut of 'Under-five' outlets springing up on every corner, this age range needs parent time, and lots of it. The hands on, everyday kind. That's the place real toddler socialisation is found. This is the bunch that responds the best to consistent nuggety love, boundaries and another generous dollop of consistency. Sadly, two-to-six-year-olds, currently, are the group most likely to be pacified with as minimal direct attention an adult can get away with.

From one parent to another...

Over a year and a half ago, I was teaching children's choir, teaching adult education classes two nights a week, singing in the adult choir, four children underfoot, taking the children two full days a week to extra classes, preparing to move to a new location... and running a website as a business. I was overwhelmed!

One night I walked into our six-year-old daughter's room and saw a basket hanging from her bunkbed with a stuffed animal and a note in it. I remembered that Brittany had told me she had a surprise for me, and to please come and look at it, but I was too busy filling an order for my business. Later, after I sent her to bed, she called me again to see her surprise, but I said was still too busy and I'd come when I could.

Much later in the evening, I remembered that I had never gone back to see Britty's surprise. Feeling a little saddened that I was seeing it after she was asleep, I opened the note.

On it was written: 'I want to do 100 things for you.'

For Brittany, a brand-new 6 year old who had four ear surgeries, writing that note would have been very difficult. It touched me to the core. In tears, I said aloud, 'I want to do 100 things for you, too.'

It was as if a light turned on in that moment as I saw how busy I had made my life. Each activity was noble, of course, and worthy of someone's time, but it was not to be my time that was used.

That night, in my little girl's room, I felt God's whisper. I heard Him whisper that I am to be first a wife, then a mother for this moment. He reminded me how quickly children grow up. It is only for a blink of time that they live with us.

With my focus cleared, I immediately closed my website. Since we were moving, I was able to gracefully bow out of choir, children's choir, the extra classes, and teaching commitments.

I started caring whether or not my husband had clean clothes. Our children also became a higher priority. I started reading to them at night and singing with them in the day. I focused on their little faces and the fun we could create together. The

house also became a priority. With practice, it became a joy while teaching our children how to manage a home happily.

If we young mothers talked to older mothers more often, they'd tell us that children grow up quickly. We already know that, but do we realise it? We fill our days to overflowing with activities; we run after new challenges; we start new businesses or keep old jobs; we agree to fill rotas, take on new roles.

Meanwhile, our families are set aside.

Lori Seaborg,
www.homeschoolblogger.com/KeepingtheHome

Hot potato: Don't bend the wire

The pull of a kid to other kids is the greatest magnetic pull I've come across. Kids love being with other kids. The downside to this reality is that, given a free rein, they may magnetise towards other kids who are bursting at the seams with attitudes and behaviours you want nothing to do with. One father told me that he lay awake at night just knowing that his daughter was going to slip over to the murky smog of teenage culture and there was nothing he could do but watch her thrashing around. Is that the reality? Is a parent's role in the whole issue of peers as irrelevant as an over 50s' discount night at a top nightclub? Are boundaries redundant when they're past the squabbling-over-toys stage? The aim of good parenting is not to keep the kids sweet. If something just doesn't sit right with you, don't get talked around. Boundaries may just save their life (in more ways than the obvious).

From one parent to another...

A few months ago I took Jason (14) out to lunch. Actually, he suggested it and he was buying so off we went to Arby's. While I watched him eat his four sandwiches in the length of time it took me to eat one, we chatted about a lot of different things. When there was a lull in the conversation I asked him if we still retained his heart even though he was in the middle of growing from a boy to a man.

He grinned and said, 'Mom, if you and dad didn't have my heart then do you think I'd be sitting here with you at Arby's right now?'

Good point.

So I pressed him a little on why he thinks teens seem to stray away and what could a parent do to keep a child from rebelling.

He said, 'Don't bend the wire.' I was confused. What exactly does that mean?

He kept going. 'Did you ever notice that a wire once it has been bent can't go exactly straight again. I've tried it. It can go pretty straight but you can never get the kink out completely.' Now, I was really confused and wondering if my son really understood what I was getting at.

I asked him, 'What does any of this have to do with you and teenagers?'

'Mom,' he said, 'you and dad are the wire and I am trying to get you to bend a little but don't do it. Don't give in to my selfish demands. I may recover but it will never be quite the same. Most parents don't understand that we want you to say no. The minute you give in it's all over. I want to believe what you believe but if you don't believe in it why should I?'

I got it.

This is from a son who was very difficult to handle at different times. The son who in his early years could send me into tears just by walking into the room. Now he was sitting across from me and telling me to stay strong and stay the course. I am sure there will be a few more bumps in the road before he takes on the full responsibilities of a man but I am following his wise counsel and I think he is going to make one fine husband and father one day.

Karen Braun, www.spunkyhomeschool.blogspot.com

NOW matters. One day, very soon, our window of parenting will close and their lives will be forever blessed (or hampered) by the boundaries we set (or didn't)...

How to win the 'WHY is it always me?' argument

Perhaps the biggest hot potato between a mum and a dad is the argument about who is doing more than their fair share of the parenting chores. This is one of the most argued-over issues between parents and certainly deserves its place in the 'parenting hot potatoes wall of fame'.

Let's lay the cards on the table... Despite paternity leave, men doing night feeds and some jolly decent guys out there on the fathering front, there is still one clear winner on the 'who primarily looks after the kids?' stakes – the answer is mama. If you're still reading this through slitted, sceptical eyes, let me lay my cards on the table for you. Guys are able to go for more than 30 minutes or even a couple of hours without their parent role sneaking up behind them and shouting in their ear. Mums, however, have the parental urge tugging away all day long, however neatly it is stashed away. It's there bubbling away, 24/7. Mama is armed with the tools of the trade from hugs to sticky paracetamol syrup, and she busts the ghost every time. I can do the whole 'sponging a feverish child, reading *Thumbelina* till they fall back asleep' routine while my husband is still doing the zombie walk around the kitchen looking for a medicine spoon.

All of this 'unfairness' leaves us with two possible options. First, the universal parenting 'hot potato' that whispers, 'It's not fair that I'm doing all the work around here!' Then a deeper whisper reminds us that maybe parenting is the most jaw-dropping precious time of life, and we're all the more honoured to have a bigger piece of it. This parenting journey is full of twists and turns; parenting will cost us along the way. Don't resent the hard graft that happens in between the priceless moments.

The hard graft of parenting is pain and pleasure all rolled into one; boy, do you know it if ever this role gets temporarily suspended. When my newborn daughter was five days old, my oldest son Joseph trapped his finger in a faulty door at school. The school secretary rang up in near hysteria. (I like to think this was due to my son's finger being held on by a tendon, not that we could sue the pants off them for having a faulty door.) Well, within 2.6 seconds of receiving the call I had my shoes on ready to go rescue my howling son from the limp clutches of the high-pitched secretary. My Supermama suit was zipped up, rocket boosters charged, mama ninja was coming! Then a tiny kitten mew of a cry came from newborn Miranda and I made a split-second decision that she would have to come with me on my rescue mission. Hysterical school secretary lady would just have to let me into the school office with car seat and baby paraphernalia. Nothing was going to stop Supermama. Well, my husband then wisely pointed out that it was impossible to handle a ravenous newborn and wailing five-year-old with his finger hanging off at the same time. Plus the emergency room might not appreciate a trail of breast milk wherever I went. So, 'Superdaddy' set off to the school instead. He did a most spectacular recover-and-rescue mission without even a hint of the attitude I would have given hysteria woman and her dodgy doors. I'll hold my hand up here and say that, while it tore me apart to not be with Joseph at such a traumatic time, the experience cemented a 'Daddy's my hero' in the heart of my boy.

When all is said and done...

'Parenting hot potatoes' are tricky issues which do affect the way our families go forward. The issue of outsourcing parenting is perhaps the biggest hot potato we have to face. Childcare insitutions may keep our children entertained and educated, but this is nothing compared to quality time with someone who loves them. Only today I heard that our local school is soon to offer evening meals on site and regular health checks in school hours. Sure, there may be a tiny minority of kids who would otherwise go without an evening meal or health check. Yet, the reality is these facilities are a convenient resource for parents, enabling them to hand over even more of the parenting role. It makes life easier for the hard-pressed parent. I question whether this philosophy has any benefit to the child. I am passionate about this as I think outsourcing parenting will cost dearly in the lives of the future generation.

The 'hot potato' issue of 'stranger danger' means many of us are wary of branching out into the community and allowing people in our neighbourhood one-on-one time with our children. While we must always be alert to potential risks for our children, this shouldn't cause us to cocoon them from genuine members of our communities who would love to be part of our lives. Heritage from one generation to the next will be lost if we don't give opportunity. The next 'hot potato' we discussed was 'Don't bend the wire'. This is a phrase coined by a teen to explain that, actually, teens really want boundaries to be kept. Arguing teens are a huge 'hot potato' in many families; here is a reminder that keeping our boundaries brings security. Our final 'hot potato' was the cry of the burnt-out parent: 'Why is it always me?' The only answer to this is to embrace parenting without resentment, regardless of other people's involvement. This decision can be one of the hardest we may make, and our children will be blessed beyond measure by a mama who chooses not to resent her lot in life.

8

Having it all – is it really possible?

Occasionally, I can be caught daydreaming about how my kids will grow to be fine young adults, happy and confident in their world. I imagine opening our front door to grown kids and their spouses. I picture huge Christmas parties, pebble-dashed with joyous laughter. Many a time I've reckoned that if we make it to that day, then I'll be happy. I'd have done my job. My tinsel bubble, however, keeps getting burst with one annoying reality that I finally must face: As intrinsically we are bound to our children's future, our lives are still a separate entity. We can't live today on the assurance of future happiness credits. This, however, doesn't stop us die-hard jugglers trying for the jackpot in the happiness stakes anyway. It's not just our kids' future happiness we're after, we're aiming for happy life in all departments. To many of us, that's what 'having it all' is all about. Before we dive into whether 'having it all' is possible, or indeed desirable, let's get a couple of basics covered first. Check out the three 'notes' below that discuss: the prospect of 'having it all' for when life takes a turn for the worse; the long-term feasibility of 'having it all'; whether organisation is actually the key to 'having it all'.

A note for the days when life doesn't work out as expected

OK, so digging Polly Pockets accessories out of the toilet bowl wasn't my idea of a fun Saturday morning. Nor was sleeping with a kid's foot in my face all night, then going downstairs for breakfast to find the little darling has swiped all the chocolate-coated Cheerios. Humph! Life with kids, there is no doubt, can be a messy business. Nevertheless, I know I'd be lost without knowing that my kids just long for a night-time cuddle with me. I love being the only one who knows where the kids keep their diaries and I love being privy to the Narnia game my youngest has made up. These priceless gems are the gold dust of Parentland. To your kid, you are the one who can fix all wrongs, solve all arguments; their very existence depends on our presence. However, we shouldn't kid ourselves that 'having it all' means we are actually infallible and invincible. We can't predict the journey our life will take, but I'd bet my spa gift voucher that there will always be something unexpected behind the next corner. We are so not doing ourselves any favours by perceiving that we MUST be a tower of strength and hold everything together whatever happens. There are those that just can't bear the thought that the world might come crashing down without them. Juggling is an addiction, a way of keeping control. Some women struggle even to let their husbands look after the kids for a morning. It is good to realise that we are not actually the complete masters of our destinies, planning and scheduling the way through. Life is a wild exhilarating ride, full of twists and turns. Plenty of highs and some lows on the way. Surely a big part of raising strong kids is tooling them up to realise that mummy and daddy can't immediately fix any problem that might emerge on the journey. Surely a big part of cherishing ourselves is realising that some things will be too big to handle on our own. I don't want to burst the glittery 'have it all' bubble before we've even got started, but I'd rather be real. We don't have all the answers. A goal of 100 percent sheer family happiness is unrealistic; sometimes we just have to hang on in there, hold tight to each other and ride the bumps.

A note for the days when you want something to show for all your work

You can't beat the feeling of having something to show for all the work, energy and time we put in. I've a sneaking suspicion that when our effort doesn't produce tangible results, we're tempted to juggle another area of life that gives immediate results, just so we feel as if we've achieved something. The problem with family life is that much of a parent's effort and love doesn't produce clear, immediate results. 'Pats on the back' are hard to come by, and self-sacrifice is often on the agenda. Even the satisfaction of an organised home is short-lived when whirlwind kids and their friends touch down. There's many a parent who has mumbled (or yelled) 'What's the point?'

There are some things that are impossible to describe – the smell of wet grass, the sound of snow falling, the feel of wind on your cheek. Yet they are real and less fleeting than many of the more tangible 'results' in our world. We live in a cookie-driven society; 'results' are the quick-fix cookies that many thrive on. However, I am now certain that results-chasing simply doesn't deliver satisfaction. When it comes to families, we need the wisdom of a master gardener to keep nurturing, feeding, clipping, protecting and watering till the summer comes. It's about building for the long term, not just focussing on the here and now.

A note about organisation: The key to 'having it all'?

If I'm in a bookstore and I pick up a book on organisation, I find myself stuffing the book back on the shelf quicker than you could flick a duster at me. Not because I don't believe in organisation, but because the 'picking up, putting away' charade already seems to consume so much of my time. The last thing I want to read is a book that will make me feel even more guilty and obsession-driven than I already do! Also, I'm slightly suspicious that I might get lured into a world where buffing up your suite gives a real thrill and reorganising your understairs cupboard leaves you breathless. So I stuff the book back on the shelf and pick up a cute diary instead.

Throughout this book we have discussed the importance of initiating positive steps for our families, ditching life's baggage, rebooting a child's self-esteem and imagination. If you're on the quest to make these a reality, these issues require action, effort, change and consistency. So, despite my resistance to treating families like projects to be organised, the reality is that organisation must be part of the picture to cement these good things for a lifetime. So let's put organisation under the spotlight as to its value in the quest to build a great family.

Scheduling, life planning, call it what you will. There's no doubt that there is a certain satisfaction in ticking a tick box on a list. Even more satisfying, perhaps, than successfully pulling off pretending to be asleep when a child squeals for attention just as your husband is getting into bed. Many parents swear by organisation as the very elixir of life, the oil that makes the cogs of life turn, the thinking woman's tool to 'having it all'. Whatever your stance, we all know that without some sense of organisation the day very easily tumbles into chaos and somehow things just don't get done. That's the bottom line. Now, we're considering the role of organisation in a quest to 'have it all'. The crux of the issue is to answer these questions: Is organisation a tool or master? Is it a way of being controlling? Am I trying to grab life by the throat and force things to go my way? When organisation is more than a simple tool in life, satisfaction will never come. The true value of organisation is that it enables prioritising, self-discipline and planning of the good stuff in life. When positive choices are made in a family, it's the organisational skills that help us cement these new skills into habits that last a lifetime.

So, we've explored a few key issues surrounding the concept of 'having it all'. Now for the really good stuff; time to lay a great foundation that will last a lifetime.

'Having it all' – laying a great foundation

If 'having it all' means long-term happiness and stability, then building a great marriage is the foundation to build. Lifetime commitment is undisputedly the best foundation on which to build a family. Worldwide research shows that kids thrive in this environment. They have happier, more successful lives, scoring higher socially and academically than children of non-married parents. There is also no denying the reality that life may deal unexpected blows and some of us find ourselves out of this 'ideal' marriage scenario. Life can be very harsh, and sometimes we make regretful choices. In this situation it can be really hard to read about the 'ideal' base for family life, if your situation is different. Nevertheless, this doesn't change the reality that lifetime commitment is the best hope for family life of the future, and we should uphold and cherish this institution.

Foundation 1: The slime and sparkle of marriage

Every mother, upon giving birth, is also endowed (I believe) with a kind of tolerance generator. We use it 24/7 when our kids are toddlers so we have the patience to endure a ketchup-throwing, homemade-food-refusing, wallpaper-eating little cherub. Then one day, if we're not careful, our tolerance generators turn on us and we find ourselves merely 'tolerating' everyone in our world. In my experience this can be the silent killer that can creep up on even the happiest marriages. Being in a 'tolerating each other' relationship doesn't have the shock factor of explosive arguments, but it's just as dangerous. Merely tolerating someone devalues who they are and what they mean to you. It's like a shiny car, rusting away under the bonnet.

OK, it's confession time again.... When we first had kids I acted like I had the monopoly on parenting, and he was just tagging along for the ride. Kind of like when the kids dragged me on a pirate ship ride at the theme park. I was up there – whooping it up with the kids and he was watching, waving each time we swooped past. I secretly reckoned that I was up to speed on parenting and he could actually do with pulling his socks up. My evidence? Well, he feigned interest in my reading a paragraph of a parenting book to him (when I just knew that he was mentally winning the 'fastest finger first round' of *Who Wants to be a Millionaire?*). I thought I knew it all.

Men don't wake up at night sweating whether to buy a Winnie the Pooh birthday cake or attempt a homemade creation with yellow icing. They see the bigger picture rather than the details. The same parenting ingredients are there; they just don't see everything through mama-tinted glasses. Many women see this difference as a weakness and take it upon themselves to start making improvements on a man's parenting skills. The result of giving him tips and nudges is that his sense of being a good dad get crushed. The woman's 'encouragement' is actually fully blown manipulation. Do this for a while, and BANG you've got a whiney wife, resentful husband, confused kids. Before you know it, the glistening castle of a family life turns out to be made of nothing stronger than icing. An icing castle looks good, but it melts in the heat. The conclusion? Merely tolerating your man, or manipulating him, will chip away at the foundation of your family. Quite simply, these attitudes have to be ditched if you want to build a great marriage.

Foundation 2: How to win the 'who's had the hardest day' argument

'Running the gauntlet' is a sport derived from medieval times when an assault course of swinging daggers, disappearing floors and swinging boulders was set up. The aim being to knock the contender over as he tries to race through to win the prize. Upon making it through, bashed and bleeding, he is met with cheers, honours, prizes and grapes. Now take an average mum's day – feeding, clothing, nappy changing, shopping, working, argument diffusing, moral guidance, humping the turbo vacuum, pulling off a career... If that's not a modern day gauntlet I don't know what is! So we reach the end of the day, and we're looking forward to maybe a cheer or grape or two... what if it doesn't happen? Humph! In the world of parents this 'humph' is big, and it rests on a need to be understood, appreciated. Just as, indeed, our mate needs also to feel. If this particular need is not met, on either side, life can soon feel quite pointless. The crucial point here is that disillusionment flourishes when we look for our own needs to be met first. A family needs shape, direction, roles...

From one parent to another

When we first moved into this area eleven years ago, I commented to my husband about how beautiful a certain tree looked down the road. He glanced at it and quickly assessed the situation much differently than I did. 'The tree is beautiful now but give it a few years and it won't be so nice.' What did he see that I didn't see?

A few feet above the base of the tree there were two strong limbs going in separate directions. My husband rightly pointed out that unless one of the two main limbs was pruned the tree would eventually split apart. The tree was developing two leaders. Over the years I watched the tree. After a storm, the tree would always lose a few more limbs. The tree began to look more haggard and beaten. Eventually, it didn't look at all like when I first saw it. Just two weeks ago, the tree split in half and had to be removed.

Our family was the same way. Nice looking on the outside but we had a fundamental problem in the structure. This family had two leaders, he and I pulling different directions. Here are some of the things I've now learnt.

A family cannot have two leaders. Eventually, the strength of the family is weakened and in the worst cases a split occurs. That is not to say that this is the only cause of divorce but it is definitely a problem. A house divided against itself cannot stand. The children are the limbs of a tree. When the tree is strong, the limbs remain firmly attached. But a weak tree will produce weaker limbs. I am a major branch in the tree but not the leader. My primary role is to be the best supporting limb for my husband so that he can provide direction and not have to struggle with me. As a result, the whole family prospers.

The fear that my husband wouldn't lead our family was very strong. What would happen then?

And there were times when I was tempted to take over.

We are always being pruned. There is never a point at which the process ends and we become the 'perfect family'.

A final story. During the Christmas holiday season a few years ago I had made a list of things to do to get ready for Christmas Day. As I set out the Saturday before Christmas to work through my list ... I felt prompted to ask Steve if he needed my help. He had decided to wash the floors and carpets that day. Not a favourite job of mine, so I was glad to see him doing it. Grateful for my help, he asked if I would go to the store and buy a few more scrub brushes. It was the busiest shopping day of the year, and going out was the last thing I wanted to do! I had already made my list of things to accomplish. How were they ever going to get done?

A part of me wished I had never asked. But I went. And what should have been a 30 minute trip took nearly 2 hours. When I got back home, he asked if I would mind helping him scrub for a while. 'Why no honey, of course not.' (I was thinking something totally different!) So I had to once again set aside my plans. At this point everyone was in on the action. What child doesn't love bubbles and a chance to make a floor soaking wet in the middle of winter? I began to relax a little and enjoy the moment.

As we were scrubbing, my eight year old daughter Katie came up and whispered, 'Momma, do you know what? We have a happy home.'

Karen Braun, www.spunkyhomeschool.blogspot.com

Exploding two myths about 'having it all'

Myth 1: 'Happiness is just around the corner'

Some parents are reaching so high in aspects of their life that they forget to actually enjoy the ride on the way. So our first myth that we are going to explode is the one that whispers 'Happiness is just around the next corner.' It's all very well reaching for the stars in all areas of life, but if that's not based on a contentment with what I already have, however small, happiness will forever elude me. The word 'contentment' has had bad press. It makes us think of a timid wife satisfied with darning a few socks and mopping the floor. We may perceive that role as pitiful, oppressive. Well, I think it's time that we took a whole new look at the concept of contentment in the 21st century. The contemporary culture is anything but content. It is forever chasing the next new thing, never focussing on one thing for very long. Well, I think that way of living is, at its core, unsatisfying. Maybe a touch of contentment is something our world is sorely missing.

Here's a snippet of 'contentment' wisdom from a friend of mine, Spunkyjunior (age 16).

> Economics hasn't been my favourite subject this year ... After reading a few pages, my book introduced the idea of needs and wants. People *need* things and people *want* things. Amazingly, I actually started to enjoy it!
>
> Needs are unlimited. Our needs are usually fewer than our wants.

**That's obvious. My wish list of wants is huge...
Want... need... want... It's a never ending cycle. I spy
a new camera, better than the one I have, and it
immediately becomes a want. If all my socks have
holes in them and I know winter is creeping closer,
then getting socks is a need. But I don't find myself
dreaming about new socks all day! But cameras...
now I'm dreamin'. I've got a 'wanting' attitude... I
am not content until my want turns into a purchase.
Thankfully, I have learnt over time not to buy on
impulse. That may keep my money safe, but my
attitude still needs adjusting. God has been teaching
me contentment lately. It hasn't been fun and I'm
learning it the hard way!**

Kristin Braun, www.spunkyjunior.blogspot.com

Myth 2: 'Satisfaction comes from having a busy life'

The second myth that we are going to explode is the one
that says we must have many busy facets of life in order
to have a full and satisfying life. Life may be bursting at
the seams with positive activity but does that
automatically bring happiness? I'll be honest, I get a real
buzz from activity. I love being involved in all sorts of
things. Yet I wonder sometimes if the lure of something
new is really a poor substitute for genuine satisfaction
and contentment.

Yesterday my turbocharged family and I went for a
day trip at an indoor snow experience centre. I was
booked for two hours of snowboarding lessons, which I
confess were booked by me in a hasty moment of 'let's try
something new'. I had quite a thrill in the days running

up to the event dropping out mid-conversation about our adventurous sporting endeavours. This, I decided, was us making the most out of life. Extreme sports? Bring it on! Tooling up in snow gear, I ignored the fact that I can't even stay upright on my kid's scooter, and that I'm not great with heights. Oh yes, and it also slipped my mind that I slightly freak out if my feet are pinned down. Somehow these realities didn't even engage. I queued up in anticipation behind the surf bum in a ski jacket so electric blue it made my fillings tingle. It wasn't until I was on a very slippery slope, knuckles white and jelly legs frozen in fear, that I had the urge to drop to my hands and knees and crawl along like I feel like doing on very high bridges. Add to this a snowboarding instructor, teeth reflecting the snow, chuckling to himself. 'You a snow virgin? Eh?' And the urge to hobble off quietly suddenly became far more overwhelming than the urge to be a snow sports master. Sure, trying new things and meeting new people is fun. However, don't be mistaken that this buzz is what life is all about. The buzz is great while it lasts, but it is not the answer to having a full and satisfying life. Busyness is the best excuse in the world for not actually sifting through our juggling balls and seeing what's worth having, and what's not worth the effort.

So, we've discussed some key issues around the concept of having it all. We've identified the best foundation to lay, we've exploded a few myths. Read on for how to prioritise the chunks of your life, get those juggling balls in order. How do we sift through the balls so only the precious make it to the juggling basket?

The crux of it all

Now here's a thought. Maybe juggling is only what we are doing with all the chunks of our life. Successfully juggling doesn't make any particular chunk worth having, it's just keeping them in the air. I'm leaning towards the conclusion that successful juggling of all the balls, while possible, is NOT the answer to having a great family life. The real question is in the choices we make in deciding what balls to have in our family basket in the first place. Questioning these choices is not an easy thing to do, so most jugglers pop them on the back burner and head back on to the hamster wheel for another quick whiz around.

Hamsters have many tricks up their sleeves... one is that they're convinced that given a wheel they will get somewhere. Make something great of their life. No one could doubt a hamster's enthusiasm, drive and effort. Yet they get nowhere. Do they get off the wheel, reassess, and put their activities into something with results? No. Because the wheel is familiar and the rush of wind whistling past convinces them they are achieving great things... bounding to a sweaty victory at the hamster marathon.

Sifting through the balls of life

The best place to 'sift through the balls' of life is, of course, with a fine latte and a wonderful sea view. If you don't have this to hand, you may have to make do with a mug of steaming tea and a kitchen table like me. Then I got a piece of paper and drew a large circular cake (keeping with the coffee shop theme!). I drew my circle, then I divided my cake into all the 'slices' that my life is made up of. There were more slices than I realised! I identified the slices that were poor quality, life sapping rather than life building. Then, I decided to ditch them from my life. My daughter no longer goes to nursery, I've stepped down from a club that was stressful much of the time, I've chosen to improve my time management. You see, this book was written, not by an ex-juggler who had found all the answers, but by a girl burnt out to a crispy pretzel with relentless juggling. This book has been my real journey.

I guess it's no surprise to you that the juggling balls that I've chosen to keep are: devotion to my husband; nurturing and inspiring my kids; challenging myself to grow and flourish in my passions, and being a team player with the others in my world. Sure, a 'career ball' of being an author is in the juggling basket right now. But if this 'career ball' stole oxygen from my priority balls, I would let it completely go. The family balls I hold are just too precious to leave around in the basket for someone else to juggle. By prioritising, I've renewed my time energy for the stuff that really matters. It wasn't easy! I do, however, feel lighter; the balls I now juggle feel less like sandpaper, more like velvet.

Standing by my post

When I'm at the cinema and the credits roll, this sentence always catches my eye: 'THIS FILM IS NOT BASED ON PERSONS LIVING OR DEAD'. This, I guess, is so we can't sue the nuts off the film companies. I assume this also means that a fair bit of imagination and effort goes into creating entirely fabricated characters. Well, I would have the imagination to fabricate the people I'm about to tell you about, but I'm afraid my kids used up all my imagination juice playing ice monsters. So, I'll just have to use real examples...

I have a friend in marketing and she's always coming out with cutting-edge phrases like, 'Well I had such a blue sky moment...' I confess that instead of cocking my head to one side and saying 'What are you getting at?' I nod my head enthusiastically and 'mmm' in agreement. All her verbal hopscotch makes me feel like my conversation is quite dull, a reality I entirely attribute to playing Thomas the Tank Engine for four solid years. I could hold an enamoured debate about the subtle differences between diesels and steam engines but there just doesn't seem to be much call for this area of expertise. One phrase that she says, however, has struck a chord with me. It is 'standing by your post'. She uses this phrase to mean 'keeping with your original plan'.

This phrase, however, did not originate in a marketing mumbo-jumbo manual or even military phrase book. It originated, I believe, as some costly words uttered by a woman 250 years ago. A young family travelled for months across dusty terrain to find a place where they could build a home and make a living. It was a long, exhausting journey that they barely survived. The mother fed and nurtured her little ones; she supported her husband in his venture. She was inspired by stories of a new life where they could build a home and live freely, earn a living, and worship without persecution. Finally they reached a clearing and began to set up a small home. A passing traveller stopped for dinner and promised to take a note to their family saying that they had finally arrived. Then, that night, when the man of the house was out hunting, locals came by looking for loot. They were angry at the family's intrusion on the bush. So they tied the mother up, said they would untie her animals, and then kill her. In the brief moments she had, the mother said to the messenger, 'Tell my sister, I know what it is to live. Now I die at my post.'

She knew that living life to the full is not about having the perfect life or even achieving goals. She knew that there was more to life. This is also the very essence of my every heartbeat: Being a Christian, for me, is not about being a do-gooder, or a traditionalist. These things I am not. I'm not expecting a goody bag of blessings to fall into my lap; I am no better than the next person. For me, it's about the reality that the one who flung the stars into space actually calls me, Jane, his beloved. I run like the wind when I hear his voice. I just reckon a sunset; the birth of a baby; a flower; the passions in my heart are evidence of a world that was lovingly created, not an accident. DNA doesn't just tumble into place to create the amazing kids that we spend our lives with. Our kids are unique, and they were made on purpose. Intrigued? The book of John in the Bible might just catch your eye. Now, I know why I'm on this planet.

And I too will live and die at my post.

9

Around the kitchen table...

This chapter is bursting at the seams with parenting stories written by mums like you. Pour yourself a huge mug of hot chocolate with some sprinkly bits on top, and enjoy these great heartwarming stories...

One morning, my kids were playing outdoors while I cleaned the kitchen. My youngest son, who was two at the time, came in and announced, 'Mom, I put Rusty in the hole.'

'Oh?' I asked, casually continuing to wipe a plate.

'Yeah, he's in the hole.'

'Okay,' I said. I wasn't really alarmed, because the kids played with the hamster all the time.

Soon the older boys came in, and Levi shared the news that he'd put Rusty in the hole. 'What hole?' they asked him.

And then the trouble started.

'In the car,' Levi said.

'THE CAR? Where in the car?'

'In the hole,' he patiently explained, a little louder this time, as if we were all idiots.

'Okay, guys, let's go see where he is,' I said, and we all

trooped out to the car. Levi went around the back, and pointed... to the tailpipe.

'He's in there,' he said.

For the next two hours, we tried to get him out. We talked to him. We tried banging on the pipe. Once or twice we saw his little pink nose, but the pipe was too small for me to reach my hand in to get him. I put some hamster food at the end of the pipe. Then we tried cereal. I should have tried calling the pizza delivery hamster that used to deliver to his 'pad' in the hall closet. Anyway, after a couple of hours, we had to run an errand in our other vehicle. Afraid he'd escape only to be eaten by a neighbourhood cat, I taped off the end of the tailpipe with some masking tape. (Yes, I left some space so air could get in – what do you think I am, stupid?) When we returned, the food we'd put in was gone, but the masking tape was still there, so apparently Rusty was, too.

By the time my husband returned from work it was dark out, and Rusty was still in the tailpipe. I was starting to worry, and the kids were pretty frantic. We couldn't think of anything else to try. Then, Daddy had a brilliant idea:

Start the car.

At this point, I was convinced that we'd never get him out anyway, and he'd get stuck somewhere up in the engine or something, and with it being hot here and all, well... it wasn't going to be pretty.

My middle child (the actual owner of the hamster) stood behind the car holding a kitchen strainer. The other kids stood on either side, looking on in trepidation. I went inside because I couldn't bear to watch. Daddy got in the car and started it.

Out shot Rusty, flying over and six feet past the strainer. He landed at the end of the driveway, dazed and covered in soot. His little hamster eyes were looking at us, like, 'What on earth was that???'

The boys brought him in to me with their hands black from the powdery ash covering him. I knew we couldn't leave all that stuff on him, so I put him in the sink and broke out the strawberry-scented Suave shampoo. In the sink, he shrank to one quarter of his normal size and looked like, well, a drowned rat, honestly. So to add insult to injury, I blew him dry with my hair dryer.

Rusty was never really the same after that, though remarkably he did live for another several years. He mostly stayed home and ran on his wheel. Apparently, he'd seen enough of the world.

Misty Krasawski, www.homeschoolblogger.com/MistyKrasawski

Real moms...

- Never dust. Real moms know that the best way to keep furniture dust-free is to let the kids climb on it.
- Pretend that they are deaf when they hear 'she pinched me' or 'he frowned at me'. Unless there are blood-curdling screams or actual blood, the real mom knows not to get involved.
- Never wax the kitchen floor. Real moms know the only wax that belongs on a floor is that from a stepped-on crayon.
- Visit the bakery section of the grocery store to bribe her crew with cookies before the shopping begins. She is careful to get enough sweet stuff

such that their mouths are full for the entire trip.

- **NEVER** have an uninterrupted phone conversation.
- Never eat a hot meal. By the time they get everyone else fed, the food is cold.
- Never use the bathroom without an audience. Her make up and feminine products are found around the house being used to create interesting construction projects.
- Know that no matter what happens, these crazy days will all be a memory one day and she will end up longing for these days to return.
- Try not to take things too seriously because things could be a lot worse.

Victoria Carrington, www.homeschoolblogger.com/
victoriacarrington

'Arf! Arf!' The little red dog chases my 17 month old son around the house and he squeals with delight. The dog gives kisses and buries his head into Brehane's neck. There is laughter all over the place. Even the dog laughs. How, you may wonder, can a dog laugh? You see, the dog is a stuffed animal, and I am the voice. So as I laugh, the dog does the same.

It is so amazing how using a bit of imagination can brighten a child's world. To look at my son light up as he does when we play a pretend game of 'Doggie Chase Brehane' is such a joy. At that moment, in that window of time, Brehane allows his imagination to take him to another place. As a matter of fact, we go there together.

Chasing him around the house and tickling him with

the red dog, reminds me that it is good to 'play pretend'. As adults, we tend to get away from the fun in life. We allow ourselves to get caught up in the rut of life, rather than enjoying the abundance that it has to offer. The innocence we once knew becomes clouded by the demands of life. Many of us just don't know how to have fun anymore.

While it is important to work and take care of our tangible needs, it is just as important that we learn to play a bit. Sometimes we have to throw caution to the wind and have a good time.

As mothers, we have much that can tear us down. The challenges that we face seem insurmountable at times. We are wives, mothers, sisters, friends, doctors, psychologists, cooks, maids, managers, and so much more. It is hard to smile when so much stands before us and depends on us for survival. Now, I challenge you to take a moment, think about something funny and have a good laugh. Play with your kids. Get away from the monotony for a while. Let the chores rest. Order pizza tonight. Determine to have a good time.

Well, I have to go; it's time to go give the red dog another spin around the house.

La Tara Ham-Ying, www.homeschoolblogger.com/mom2boyz

Last night my baby son resisted sleep with a determination not usual to his mellow nature. I nursed him and nursed him, rocked him, laid him on my chest and patted him, but all to no avail. He didn't want to sleep. Finally, at 2.30 am, he dozed off. At 3 am, our alarm clocks rang and my husband and I got up to get him off to work. The baby stayed asleep while I fixed breakfast and packed hubby's lunch, but after I flung myself back into bed hoping for a little sleep, he began to stir, flinging his arms around as if he were conducting an orchestra, or maybe riding a dream-land bucking bronco. Ten minutes later, he was firmly awake, and spent the next couple of hours latching on and off, wiggling, fussing, and generally making a nuisance of himself. When he fell asleep again, I breathed a sigh of relief, and then, for no reason I can think of, I pressed my forehead against his sweaty brow, and lay there listening to him breathe. As I did, I forgot my frustration and my love for my sweet baby overwhelmed me, to the point where I could hardly catch my breath. Even though he was the cause of my exhaustion, my irritation faded away and was forgotten so quickly. No matter his night time habits, he's my precious little boy, full of giggles, expert in endearing himself to all of us, and so utterly wonderful that he takes his mother's breath away.

Margaret Ann Delle, www.homeschoolblogger.com/cappuccinosmom

To be honest, I actually wasn't sure that I wanted to jump on the 'bringing a child into the world' wagon. When I thought about raising children, all that came to mind was the inevitable question, 'Can I really do this and do it well?' My husband and I talked back and forth about raising a family and he finally convinced me that I would make a great mom.

Our children are now 10 and 11 years old and we have had our share of challenges. One child is hearing impaired and the other has been diagnosed with high-functioning autism/ADHD. I never envisioned that BOTH of my children would have medical issues. We have often had decisions to make regarding their care and I hope that we have made the best choices for them.

As they have grown, I have continued to doubt that I am doing a good job raising them. How many of us have wished that kids came with a 'How-to' manual at birth? Parenting a child has got to be the most incredible job in the world, but also the most frustrating at times. However, I have learned to say 'I'm sorry' when I've made a mistake and they have learned that Mom isn't perfect. It means so much to me when my kids come up to me on their own and say, 'I love you, Mom. You are the BEST mom ever!' I feel so unworthy of this compliment, probably the highest compliment a parent can receive! I guess I'm not doing such a bad job after all, huh?

Kris Price, www.homeschoolblogger.com/ClassicalEducation4Me

I have a teenage daughter. I love her very much, however at times it feels like we are from different planets. Sometimes she blinks her eyes and says, 'I love you, mommy' – translation – 'I want something'. Sometimes she looks at me with an expression that says, 'I hate you' – translation – 'I need you to understand me'.

Sometimes she stomps down the hall, borrows my things and doesn't return them. She asks me to buy ugly clothes, wants her hair streaked, her ears pierced, and would like somehow for me to alter the genetic makeup that causes her to have a nose shaped like mine and a chin shaped like her father. Sometimes she cries, and even she will readily admit it is for absolutely no reason! Recently she was really angry with someone, and when we talked it out, and dug a little deeper – I realized she wanted to stay angry at him, because she doesn't want to like him! She will ask me to sacrifice many hours of sleep to sit up and talk a problem out with her – and the very next day accuse me of never doing ANYTHING for her. She will insist I love her brother and sister more than her, that she NEVER gets a front seat in the car, that we never listen to HER music. She grumbles that she doesn't ever go ANYwhere, do ANYthing or see ANYbody – when I feel sometimes like I meet myself coming and going while helping to coordinate the social life and extracurricular activities of her and any number of her friends! She thinks herself in love with someone and talks about him 24/7, and yet rolls her eyes when her brother sings a song he likes for a second time, or I repeat a request for her music to be turned down AGAIN!

Most of the time, I would swear we don't speak the same language, and yet there is a communication that goes through to the heart. Last night she came into my bedroom crying and asked to sleep in my bed. We didn't say too many words. She just cuddled up to me, and I held her as she cried – and I thought to myself that our relationship at its core is still much like it was when she was a baby. She is still growing and changing – yet even though she thinks herself quite sophisticated and grown up, when things are hard, and the tears start to fall, she still needs me to hold her while she cries.

Julie Forsythe, www.homeschoolblogger.com/jewls2texas

I am not having a good day. Actually, it started last night when I decided to sleep in really late, just because I had half of the day off. Well, guess who woke up bright and early this morning? Yours truly. And that made me crabby, since my mind needed to sleep in even if my body didn't want to. After deciding to be crabby, I went to check for some **VERY IMPORTANT** e-mails that were supposed to be in my inbox this morning. Apparently, they were only very important to me... No one had gotten up at 6:00am to make sure their e-mails were in my inbox when I checked it at 7:30. The nerve! That made me mad and crabby at the same time! (Notice how dangerous this is getting.)

I decided to go eat some breakfast, but I had missed breakfast because I was working on my article. All that was left were a few cold scrambled eggs. I don't know if you've ever eaten cold scrambled eggs, but they're pretty gross. I went to the freezer to get a few sausages to make, only to discover they were all gone (talk about a let down) which was unbelievable, since I bought those sausages yesterday! Then my mom came around the corner with two sausage patties left over from breakfast, which I consumed with joy. My little sister complained about something, so I snapped back an irritated retort. Then my mom said, 'Why don't you grow up? You've turned a corner – backwards!' Which made me laugh, but then I got in trouble for laughing.

I went to take a shower, but discovered that I had no water pressure. I got dressed again and walked outside to find the source of the problem (the garden hose 'watering' the gravel driveway), which made me feel aggravated. Then my boss called and asked me to come to a meeting, but she wouldn't give me any details, so I was very suspicious. I drove to work and my car's air conditioner wasn't working, so I was really hot. When I got to the meeting, my two supervisors were the only people there. That set me even more on edge! Sure enough, they announced their decision to transfer me to another department, which left me feeling all mixed up!!! Do I still want to work for them? I DON'T KNOW!!!

When I got home, my very important e-mails had arrived, so I was ecstatic. I felt like blogging, but changed my mind halfway through my entry. So I left it for another day and went to bed, but I couldn't sleep because my little sister had got sand in my bed! (That speaks for itself, no need to come up with a word to describe it!) ARGH!!! Has anyone ever heard of that book 'Alexander and the no-good-awful-bad-horrible-nasty-day,' or whatever it's called? Well, I just had a day that would outrank his BY FAR!

Claire Novak, www.homeschoolblogger.com/ClaireNovak

Today I became a member of a club I didn't ask to join... a club as old as time... Its members... women all over the world, who send their children off to the military.

In less than 12 hours the van will arrive to take my child and his duffle bag off to basic training... they will drive off and he won't be my baby anymore...

He has promised to protect and defend his nation... but he is not a soldier.

He collects video games and watches the Simpsons... he loves lasagnes and garlic toast... he is a neat freak... he watches the History channel and bites his finger nails when he is nervous... his favourite Bible verse is in Mark... He's great at sports... loves to impress girls...drinks awful tasting protein shakes... and he loves his mama...

He has never played with guns... he is compassionate enough to volunteer to help the homeless...

but he is not a soldier.

When he arrives at the base they will strip him of all he is and put a gun in his hand... they will teach him warfare... the buddy system... never to leave a man behind...

He is from a small town... his father and I moved the family here to rid ourselves from the hustle and bustle of the city... to teach our boys to love nature... to have open fields to play in...

He has slept under the stars... but not in the desert... he has cooked over an open fire...but not an MRE...

He is not a soldier.

My child is asleep in his room. I peeked in on him under his comforter...this will be his last day to sleep in... Perhaps the drill-sergeants need to know he is grumpy when he first wakes up... and cranky when he is tired.

Perhaps the mess hall needs to know he doesn't like sausage... or pepper on his eggs... his skin breaks out in the cold... and he hates tags on his clothes... he loves Dr Pepper... and a warm blanket... and soft pillows... and he has a weak stomach... he'll stop and watch a sun rise...

Perhaps I should make a list... I'm sure they have their own lists...

My baby leaves... he's going to become a soldier...

Lea Eaton, www.homeschoolblogger.com/Endoftheroad

Do you have a story to share? I'd love to hear from you. Drop into www.livingheritage.org and say hello!

Jane Bullivant, May 2006